ANIMATION

■■■■■■■■■■■■■■■■■■■■■■■■■■■■■■

Drawings Spring to Life

These and other books are included in the
Encyclopedia of Discovery and Invention series:

Airplanes	Movies
Anesthetics	Phonograph
Animation	Photography
Atoms	Plate Tectonics
Clocks	Printing Press
Computers	Radar
Genetics	Railroads
Germs	Ships
Gravity	Telephones
Human Origins	Telescopes
Lasers	Television
Microscopes	Vaccines

ANIMATION
Drawings Spring to Life

by DON NARDO

The ENCYCLOPEDIA of
D·I·S·C·O·V·E·R·Y
and **INVENTION**

615285

P.O. Box 289011 SAN DIEGO, CA 92198-9011

Library of Congress Cataloging-in-Publication Data

Nardo, Don, 1947-
  Animation: drawings spring to life / by Don Nardo.

    p. cm.—(The Encyclopedia of discovery and invention)
  Includes bibliographical references and index.
    Summary: Surveys the history, development, and possible
  future of film animation, describing both traditional stop-
  motion and computer animation and discussing major
  contributors to the field.
    ISBN 1-56006-218-5
    1. Animation (Cinematography)—Juvenile literature.
  [1. Animation (Cinematography)]   I. Title.   II. Series.
  TR897.5.N37 1992
  778.5'2347—dc20
                                           92-5151
                                             CIP
                                              AC

Contents

Foreword

The belief in progress has been one of the dominant forces in Western Civilization from the Scientific Revolution of the seventeenth century to the present. Embodied in the idea of progress is the conviction that each generation will be better off than the one that preceded it. Eventually, all peoples will benefit from and share in this better world. R.R. Palmer, in his *History of the Modern World*, calls this belief in progress "a kind of nonreligious faith that the conditions of human life" will continually improve as time goes on.

For over a thousand years prior to the seventeenth century, science had progressed little. Inquiry was largely discouraged, and experimentation, almost nonexistent. As a result, science became regressive and discovery was ignored. Benjamin Farrington, a historian of science, characterized it this way: "Science had failed to become a real force in the life of society. Instead there had arisen a conception of science as a cycle of liberal studies for a privileged minority. Science ceased to be a means of transforming the conditions of life." In short, had this intellectual climate continued, humanity's future would have been little more than a clone of its past.

Fortunately, these circumstances were not destined to last. By the seventeenth and eighteenth centuries, Western society was undergoing radical and favorable changes. And the changes that occurred gave rise to the notion that progress was a real force urging civilization forward. Surpluses of consumer goods were replacing substandard living conditions in most of Western Europe. Rigid class systems were giving way to social mobility. In nations like France and the United States, the lofty principles of democracy and popular sovereignty were being painted in broad, gilded strokes over the fading canvases of monarchy and despotism.

But more significant than these social, economic, and political changes, the new age witnessed a rebirth of science. Centuries of scientific stagnation began crumbling before a spirit of scientific inquiry that spawned undreamed of technological advances. And it was the discoveries and inventions of scores of men and women that fueled these new technologies, dramatically increasing the ability of humankind to control nature—and, many believed, eventually to guide it.

It is a truism of science and technology that the results derived from observation and experimentation are not finalities. They are part of a process. Each discovery is but one piece in a continuum bridging past and present and heralding an extraordinary future. The heroic age of the Scientific Revolution was simply a start. It laid a foundation upon which succeeding generations of imaginative thinkers could build. It kindled the belief that progress is possible as long as there were gifted men and women who would respond to society's needs. When Antonie van Leeuwenhoek observed *Animalcules* (little animals) through his high-powered microscope in 1683, the discovery did not end there. Others followed who would call these "little animals" bacteria and, in time, recognize their role in the process of health and disease. Robert Koch, a German bacteriologist and winner of the Nobel Prize in Physiology and Medicine, was one of these men. Koch firmly established that bacteria are responsible for causing infectious diseases. He identified, among others, the causative organisms of anthrax and tuberculosis. Alexander Fleming, another Nobel Laureate, progressed still further in the quest to understand and control bacteria. In 1928, Fleming discovered penicillin, the antibiotic wonder drug. Penicillin, and the generations of antibiotics that succeeded it, have done more to prevent premature death than any other discovery in the history of humankind. And as civilization hastens toward the twenty-first century, most agree that the conquest of van Leeuwenhoek's "little animals" will continue.

The *Encyclopedia of Discovery and Invention* examines those discoveries and inventions that have had a sweeping impact on life and thought in the modern world. Each book explores the ideas that led to the invention or discovery, and, more importantly, how the world changed and continues to change because of it. The series also highlights the people behind the achievements—the unique men and women whose singular genius and rich imagination have altered the lives of everyone. Enhanced by photographs and clearly explained technical drawings, these books are comprehensive examinations of the building blocks of human progress.

ANIMATION

Drawings Spring to Life

ANIMATION

Introduction

Animation is a paradox. It is completely artificial—characters are drawn, animals talk, feats are performed that could never occur in real life. Yet, at its most artistic, animation is just as moving, captivating, and engaging as any real life drama, comedy, or suspense film. It seems all the more so, in fact, because it is all illusion.

Animation is the work of artists—it is their skill and imagination that can create unforgettable characters that carry on a life of their own. Nearly every child knows who Mickey, Donald, Ariel, and Thumper are—and many adults know too. This is perhaps the most marvelous thing about animation—these drawn figures seem every bit as real, every bit as concrete, as Paul Newman, Elizabeth Taylor, and Humphrey Bogart.

Animation is an art form that endures, as well. When special effects dominate movies, millions still flock to see the latest Disney film—created with the same essential technology that

TIMELINE: ANIMATION

1 ■ 1645
The magic lantern is invented.

2 ■ 1794
Phantasmagoria, a magic lantern theater, opens in Paris.

3 ■ 1824
Peter Mark Roget describes persistence of vision.

4 ■ 1877
Emile Reynaud invents the praxinoscope, the most complex of all early animation devices.

5 ■ 1892
Emile Reynaud's Theatre Optique opens in Paris. It shows animated stories using his praxinoscope.

6 ■ 1894
Thomas Edison introduces the Kinetoscope.

7 ■ 1896
Thomas Edison introduces the motion-picture projector.

8 ■ 1906
James S. Blackton makes the first animated film.

9 ■ 1914
Gertie the Dinosaur, the first film to use character animation, debuts.

10 ■ 1915-1917
Winsor McCay invents the animation cel.

11 ■ 1928
Walt Disney's Steamboat Willie is the first sound cartoon.

12 ■ 1933
Willis O'Brien animates King Kong.

launched it years ago. But people also flock to see animated films that made their debut fifty years ago—and, for the most part, they seem no less antiquated or outdated.

But animation is not just Disney, or fantasy. Every year, dozens of artists create animated short films that deliver hard-hitting political messages. These artists push the art form to accomplish more, and are somehow able to give many of the issues facing humanity today—environmental destruction, political indiscretion, and homelessness—a humorous, satirical face.

Animation is entertainment, but it seems so much more. When a child rushes up to shake Minnie Mouse's hand at Disneyland, many an adult has wished to do the same. Who would not want to believe? She seems that real.

4 > 5 > 6 > 7 > 8 > 9 > 10 > 11 > 12 > 13 > 14 > 15 > 16 > 17 > 18 > 19 > 20 > 21 >

13 ■ 1937
Walt Disney releases *Snow White and the Seven Dwarfs*, the first important feature-length cartoon.

14 ■ 1941-1945
The UPA studio begins a revolution in animation graphics.

15 ■ 1949
"Crusader Rabbit" is the first cartoon show made for TV.

16 ■ 1951
UPA's *Gerald McBoing-Boing* receives the Oscar for best animated film.

17 ■ 1960
"The Flintstones" is the first animated TV show to be broadcast in prime time.

18 ■ 1966
The TV networks launch a full lineup of Saturday morning cartoons.

19 ■ 1982
Star Trek II: The Wrath of Khan is the first feature film to utilize computer animation extensively.

20 ■ 1990
"The Simpsons," a prime-time TV cartoon show, attracts a large audience of both adults and children.

21 ■ 1990
Computer simulation is used to study the structure of a human cell.

CHAPTER 1

The Age of the Magic Lantern

The first animated films appeared at the beginning of the twentieth century. Not by coincidence, these films were produced shortly after the introduction of the motion-picture projector. Using a bright light, the projector flashes separate still pictures or drawings quickly and continuously across a screen. This rapidly changing sequence of images makes it appear as though the pictures are moving. The invention of the projector marked the beginning of an influential and entertaining worldwide movie industry. Animated films became a small but very important part of that industry.

People were fascinated with light and movement, however, long before the invention of the movie projector. For centuries, inventors and artisans experimented with devices that projected images on walls or screens for an audience's entertainment. Since most of these devices appeared before the invention of photography, the images had to be drawn. In most of these experiments, the inventors tried to simulate real life as much as possible by making the drawings move. More and more sophisticated attempts to create moving drawings eventually led to the development of animated films.

Strange Things on a Wall

A German Jesuit priest and inventor named Athanasius Kircher introduced the first important pre-animation device

Athanasius Kircher invented the "magic lantern." It projected images on a wall.

in 1645. In his book *Ars magna lucis et umbrae (The Great Art of Light and Shadow)*, he described his new invention, which he called the "magic lantern." Kircher constructed a small box with a wide hole cut in one side and placed a light source, either a candle or lamp, inside. Behind the light source, he put a curved mirror and in front of the source, a small lens. The mirror reflected the light through the lens and out of the hole in the box. Kircher placed the box on a table in a dark room. Earlier, he had painted tiny pictures on pieces of glass, or glass slides. When he positioned a glass slide in front of the hole in the box, the light passed through the glass and projected an enlarged image of the painting on a nearby wall. Sometimes the slides revolved

Such images were fairly crude. The drawings had to be small, so they did not have a lot of detail. Also, the flames in the light source flickered, causing the projected images to waver slightly. Yet the scholars and members of the nobility for whom Kircher demonstrated the magic lantern had never seen anything like it. They found it a delightful form of entertainment, and magic lanterns immediately became popular all over Europe. In 1666, British diarist Samuel Pepys described the operation of "a lanthorn [lantern] with pictures in glasse, to make strange things to appear on a wall, very pretty." Pepys was so fascinated by what he called "the lanthorn that shows tricks" that he bought one for his own use.

The next important advance in magic lantern technology occurred in 1736. A Dutch inventor named Pieter van Musschenbroek took Kircher's idea of the revolving glass disk a step further. Instead of painting separate scenes on the glass, Musschenbroek painted variations of the same scene. For example, on one disk, he sketched many drawings of a windmill. In each succeeding drawing, the arms of the mill appeared in a slightly different position. When he turned the disk quickly past the light source, the mill's arms seemed to jump from one position to another in a crude simulation of motion.

The people who witnessed Musschenbroek's demonstrations were startled and thrilled. Many wealthy Europeans invited him to their homes, where he presented elaborate magic lantern stories. Sometimes, he used two or more lanterns at the same time, each with its own revolving glass disk. This enabled him to present several images simultaneously, literally filling an entire wall with changing pictures. Another of Musschenbroek's innovations was to paint one very long picture, usually a landscape, around the entire circumference of a disk. He slowly turned the disk in front of a light source, and the landscape continuously changed before the audience. Then, he used a second lantern to project an image of an object

A page from Kircher's book The Great Art of Light and Shadow *shows how his magic lantern works.*

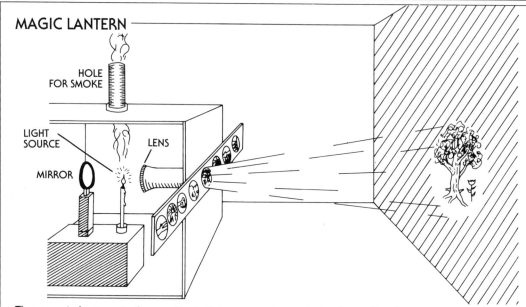

MAGIC LANTERN

HOLE FOR SMOKE

LIGHT SOURCE

MIRROR

LENS

The magic lantern is the earliest slide projector. It uses light, a mirror, and a lens to project images onto a wall or other flat surface. The same principle is still used today in overhead projectors. The magic lantern consists of a box with a small hole in the front end. A burning candle or oil lamp is placed inside the box. A curved mirror is placed behind the candle and a magnifying lens is placed in front of it. The mirror reflects the light through the lens. The lens focuses and projects the light through the hole in the box and onto the wall of a darkened room. Pictures painted on glass slides can be projected onto the wall by the magic lantern when the slide is placed in front of the hole in the box. The image can be enlarged by moving the box farther away from the wall or made smaller by moving it closer to the wall.

onto the moving image of the landscape. This created the illusion that the object was moving through the landscape. In this way, Musschenbroek was able to present complicated illusions, such as a ship passing through a storm at sea.

In the years that followed, many professional entertainers copied Musschenbroek's ideas. Some traveled from town to town, often with magic lanterns and other equipment strapped to their backs. They presented lantern shows for anyone willing to pay. Others set up permanent magic lantern theaters in major cities. The most famous and suc-cessful of these theaters was the Phan-tasmagoria in Paris, which opened in 1794. Conceived and operated by Eti-enne Gaspard Robert, who called him-self Robertson, the Phantasmagoria was the world's first horror show. Robert-son thrilled and frightened audiences by projecting images of skulls, skele-tons, ghosts, and the Grim Reaper. He achieved eerie effects by projecting the images on pieces of colored glass, sheets of semitransparent wax, or col-umns of smoke.

Like Musschenbroek, Robertson of-ten made the drawings appear to move.

Instead of windmills, Robertson painted skeletons with their arms in several different positions. When he turned the glass disk quickly in front of the light source, the arms appeared to move up and down, an effect that made audiences gasp in astonishment. Similar horror shows using this simple form of animation opened in London in 1801 and in New York City in 1803.

The characters and mechanical trickery created by Musschenbroek, Robertson, and other illusionists did more than entertain people. Magic lantern shows also inspired the young people who later became the pioneers of film animation.

Magical Toys

These early animators were also influenced by toys and other mechanical devices of the 1800s that attempted to cre-

A nineteenth-century engraving depicts the final scene from Robertson's Phantasmagoria.

ate the illusion of motion. One of the most popular animation toys was the "thaumatrope." It remains unclear who invented the device, which appeared in the mid-1820s. The thaumatrope consisted of a small disk with a different picture painted on each side. The disk was attached to strings that a person held and twirled. As the disk spun around, the pictures from the two faces of the disk appeared to combine. One of the most common thaumatropes had a painting of a bird on one disk face and a painting of a cage on the other. The spinning disk created the illusion that the bird was in the cage.

Historians believe that the idea for the thaumatrope came from observations of the visual effects produced by spinning wheels. For example, the spokes of a rapidly revolving bicycle wheel sometimes appear to move backward or forward or even stand still. British scientist Peter Mark Roget studied this phenomenon in 1824. He then published *Persistence of Vision with Regard to Moving Objects*, in which he explained an odd ability of the human eye. According to Roget, a person retains for a fraction of a second any image seen by the eye. He called this persistence of vision. If separate images flash by very quickly, he said, the eye retains the images in succession and tends to blend them together. This explained why the two images of a thaumatrope combined to form one picture. Persistence of vision makes film animation possible.

Another animation toy that became very popular in the 1800s was the "kineograph," or "flip book." The first flip books appeared in 1868, and many people claimed credit for inventing them. These toys, like the thaumatrope, depend on persistence of vision to work. A

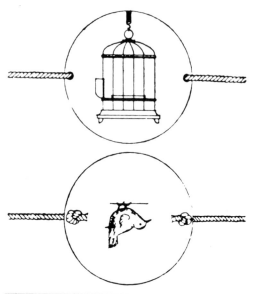

1895, American inventor Thomas Edison created a more advanced version of the flip book. His "mutoscope" was a mechanical device that flipped the pictures when the operator turned a crank. Edison had recently produced the world's first sound recordings, and the mutoscope was his attempt to blend visual images with these recordings. In other words, he was looking for a way to combine sound with realistic pictures

Thomas Edison's mutoscope flipped pictures by means of a hand crank. With his mutoscope, Edison tried to combine pictures and sound.

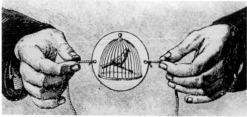

The thaumatrope demonstrates the "persistence of vision" concept. When the disk spins on the string, the eye perceives the bird to be inside the cage.

flip book consists of several dozen drawings or photographs, each part of a specific sequence of movements, bound together on one side like a regular book. Using a thumb, the operator rapidly flips the pages and the images flash by, creating the illusion of movement.

Sound and Pictures

As a sequence of drawings used to create the illusion of motion, the flip book was a direct forerunner of the animated film. The flip book was also a forerunner of the movie projector on which such films would be shown. In

the way a modern movie projector does.

In his search for a better form of visual projection, Edison was greatly influenced by the most sophisticated of all the early animation devices. This was the "praxinoscope," invented in France by Emile Reynaud in 1877. It consisted of a circular drum covered with small mirrors and turned by a crank. Around the mirrors rotated a wheel, also turned by a crank. Within the circumference of the wheel, Reynaud placed a long strip of transparent film called celluloid. He painted individual pictures on the celluloid, and these were reflected back by the mirrors. When he turned both cranks at a certain rate, the reflected images blended into each other to create an illusion of motion. Reynaud then attached a bright electric light source with its own set of mirrors and lenses that projected the images onto a white wall.

In addition to its sophisticated projection system, the praxinoscope could accommodate a roll of celluloid containing up to two thousand drawings, enough for a ten-to-fifteen-minute show. One disadvantage of the device was that it had to be cranked by hand. Therefore, the rate at which the images moved was not always uniform. Also, only one or two paintings flashed by each second. This was not enough to take full advantage of persistence of vision, and the animated images moved in a halting, less-than-realistic fashion.

Despite its shortcomings, the praxinoscope could present complete stories with bright, colorful drawings and more or less continuous movement. In 1892, Reynaud opened the elegant Theatre Optique in Paris, where he used

Emile Reynaud's praxinoscope, depicted in an engraving, presented complete stories with colorful drawings and nearly continuous motion.

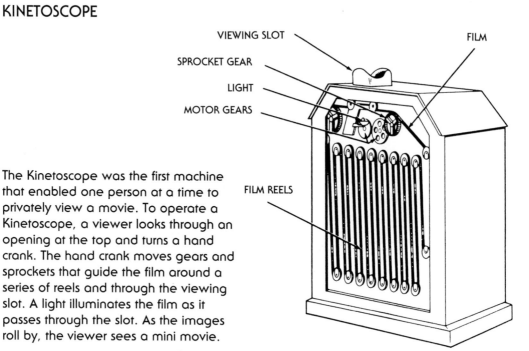

KINETOSCOPE

VIEWING SLOT

FILM

SPROCKET GEAR

LIGHT

MOTOR GEARS

FILM REELS

The Kinetoscope was the first machine that enabled one person at a time to privately view a movie. To operate a Kinetoscope, a viewer looks through an opening at the top and turns a hand crank. The hand crank moves gears and sprockets that guide the film around a series of reels and through the viewing slot. A light illuminates the film as it passes through the slot. As the images roll by, the viewer sees a mini movie.

the invention to show animated stories such as *Poor Pierrot, A Good Glass of Beer,* and *A Clown and His Dogs.* Reynaud not only ran the praxinoscope at each performance but also single-handedly completed all the thousands of drawings involved. In addition, he devised a system of music and sound effects to accompany the visuals. The Theatre Optique was so popular that Reynaud gave more than thirteen thousand performances for more than 500,000 people between 1892 and 1900. But by the end of the century, the first motion pictures, much more realistic than Reynaud's presentations, were becoming increasingly popular. Unable to compete, Reynaud went bankrupt and had to close his theater.

Meanwhile, Thomas Edison had analyzed the drawbacks of the praxinoscope and was trying to find ways to overcome them. One result of his ex-periments was the Kinetoscope, introduced in 1894. Like the praxinoscope, it used a light source, mirrors, and long strips of celluloid. But Edison put photographic images rather than drawings on the celluloid. He placed the device inside of a box with a small hole through which a person peered at the moving images. The shows were usually only a minute or less in length. Edison's peep shows quickly became popular all over the United States.

The Movie Projector

But Edison was not satisfied with simple peep shows. In 1896, he combined the elements of Reynaud's praxinoscope with elements of the mutoscope and magic lantern and added electric power to replace hand cranks. The result was

Although Thomas Edison invented the motion-picture projector in 1896, ten years passed before the projector was used to create an animated film. Edison is pictured here with one of his early projectors.

the first true motion-picture projector. The invention displayed moving images much more effectively than any of the animation toys and devices that preceded it. In Edison's projector, the images, which were recorded photographically on a long sheet of celluloid, moved steadily past an electric light source. This light produced a very bright, concentrated, and steady beam. The machine's uniform electric current ensured that the separate images, called frames, moved past the light beam at a certain rate—always sixteen frames per second. This rate took maximum advantage of the phenomenon of persistence of vision and created the illusion of natural-looking motion. A ten-minute film contained ninety-six hundred separate frames.

The movie projector, however, was more than a machine for showing moving objects. It could also make unmoving objects appear to move. Thus, it was potentially the most sophisticated of all animation devices. In a sense, it was a kind of super-praxinoscope. But most of the people who made the first motion pictures in the late 1890s, including Edison, showed little interest in the idea of film animation. The reason for this remains unclear but probably involved economics. Audiences who paid money to view the early films were fascinated by realistic, photographic images of people, animals, trains, and other things that moved. By comparison, the two-dimensional drawings used in flip books and even the praxinoscope must have seemed primitive.

Believing there was no longer a market for moving drawings, most filmmakers initially concentrated on live photography. Although all the elements needed for film animation existed, no one put them together for that purpose. After the invention of the projector, more than ten years passed before someone finally produced the first animated film.

The First Animated Films

No one person invented film animation. Once the motion-picture projector came into wide use in the late 1890s, the principles of animation became obvious to many filmmakers. But most of the early film pioneers, seeing no commercial potential for animation, did not take the idea seriously. A few filmmakers experimented with crude animation by painting tiny images directly onto frames of celluloid, much as Reynaud had done for his praxinoscope. But the quality of these images, when shown on a movie projector, was poor and unrealistic. As a result, for several years, filmmakers devoted most of their time and

energy to regular movie photography.

The first filmmaker to see the potential of film animation was a young cartoonist and entertainer named James Stuart Blackton. Born in England in 1875, Blackton was a baby when his mother brought him to the United States. Very little is known about his early life, but by the late 1880s, Blackton had already established himself as a talented artist. He managed to publish a book of drawings of seascapes while he was still a teenager. Blackton also showed a great deal of interest in acting and performing magic tricks, and he dreamed of going into show business.

After viewing a show at one of Edison's Kinetoscope parlors, J. Stuart Blackton came up with the idea of projecting images onto a screen for an audience. He was unaware that Edison was already developing a device for this purpose.

Blackton (right) used the film projector to create the illusion that inanimate drawings or objects were moving.

In 1894, Blackton attempted to make his dream come true. He teamed up with two friends, Ronald Reader and Albert E. Smith, to form a three-man magic act. They landed a few jobs performing in vaudeville theaters that featured live stage shows. In addition to magic, Blackton did extremely fast cartoon drawings of audience members and billed himself as the Komikal Kartoonist. Part of the act involved visual tricks borrowed from magic lantern shows. The three men were fascinated with these illusions as well as with those of flip books and other similar devices.

One day in 1895, Blackton and his partners viewed a peep show through one of Edison's Kinetoscopes. Instantly, they saw that the idea would have tremendous commercial potential if the images could be projected on a screen for a large paying audience. Unaware that Edison was already perfecting his own movie projector, they began working on such a device themselves. They founded the Vitagraph Company in 1896 with the goal of making and exhibiting motion pictures. Edison finished his projector first, and Blackton and the others eagerly bought several of them. They also bought cameras and began making films.

Magical Illusions

Unlike most other filmmakers of the day, Blackton was interested in animation. He believed that the magical illusions produced by the praxinoscope could be done far better using a movie projector. Blackton realized, as several other people did at the time, that the basic principle of animation was quite simple. A series of sequential drawings could be photographed one at a time, each becoming one frame of film. Or three-dimensional objects could be photographed one frame at a time, with the filmmaker moving the objects slightly between frames. In either case, when the resulting strip of film ran through a projector, the individual frames would appear to blend together. This would produce the illusion that the inanimate drawings or objects were moving.

Blackton's film The Humorous Phases of Funny Faces *combined live action and animation and is credited as being the first animated film.*

Because projectors showed sixteen frames per second, Blackton knew he would need sixteen separate drawings for every second of film. Making even a short animated film would be a time-consuming and expensive process. For years, Blackton was too busy directing and acting in his own Vitagraph films to find the time to experiment with animation.

The Birth of an Art Form

Finally, in 1905, Blackton and Smith set aside a few days to attempt some film animation. They set up their camera in front of a table, on which they placed some small wooden circus performers. Smith later wrote that the toys' "movable joints enabled us to place them in balanced positions. It was a tedious process . . . [because] movement could be achieved only by photographing sepa-

rately each change of position." Blackton and Smith named the film, which was only a minute or two long, *The Humpty Dumpty Circus*. They made only a few copies of the film, all of which were lost in the following few years. Because its existence cannot be verified, most film historians do not classify it as the first animated film. According to a later description by Smith, the animation was crude and jerky. This was because the toy figures did not bend into all the various positions that real people and animals do.

Blackton decided that he would have better control over the movements of his characters if he drew them. In 1906, he made *The Humorous Phases of Funny Faces*, now acknowledged to be the first animated film. The film was also the first to combine live action with animated drawings. For example, in one part of the film, Blackton's hand draws the faces of a man and woman. As soon as the hand moves away, the faces begin moving and changing expressions. The man blows cigar smoke at the woman, and she disappears. Then, Blackton's hand reenters the picture and erases the face of the man. Other unrelated episodes follow, including a man tipping his hat and a clown balancing on a tightrope.

Humorous Phases was only an experiment, and the animation was far from perfect. But Blackton and his partners felt that it was good enough to show as a novelty along with their other Vitagraph movies. At the time, they and other film producers showed two, three, or more short films at a time in small movie theaters around the United States. *Humorous Phases* was well received by audiences, inspiring Blackton to experiment further with animation.

Animation Becomes Popular

In 1907, Blackton made *The Haunted Hotel*, in which a man is trapped and frightened by a group of invisible ghosts. Blackton rigged his camera so that the shutter, the device that allows light to enter the camera and exposes the film, could be stopped easily after taking a single frame. He then animated objects in the hotel by photographing them one frame at a time and moving them slightly between each frame. For example, he cut a loaf of bread a little at a time, making sure that his hand and knife were out of view when the camera recorded each frame. When run through a projector at sixteen frames per second, the bread appeared to slice itself, as if by one of the ghosts. It was the same technique used earlier in *Humpty Dumpty* but executed in a much smoother and more sophisticated manner. Blackton later recalled, "What pride I took in carrying out all the weird happenings in *The Haunted Hotel*. By means of a stop mechanism on the shutter, I endowed every piece of furniture with airy animation."

Vitagraph heavily publicized *The Haunted Hotel* when releasing it to theaters. The film received widespread acclaim in the United States and Europe, prompting Blackton to produce more animated movies. For reasons that are still unclear, however, Blackton stopped making animated movies in 1910. He may have lost interest in the new art form, although it seems more likely that he became too busy to continue with such a time-consuming process. Between 1910 and 1919, he personally supervised all of the dozens of Vitagraph films produced each year. He sold Vitagraph to Warner Brothers in 1926 but later lost all of his money in bad business deals. Sadly, when he died in 1941, this great pioneer of the animated film had been forgotten by most of the filmmakers who used and profited from his ideas.

A Love for Drawing

James Blackton had introduced the new medium of animated film and proved that there was an audience that would pay money to see these films. But his stories and animation techniques remained simple, and he showed little interest for developing characters audiences liked or could identify with. The man who picked up where Blackton left off was Winsor McCay. In the span of only thirteen years, McCay single-handedly developed most of the basic techniques and devices that animators would use for generations to come.

Born in Michigan in 1867, McCay studied drawing and painting as a young man. He had an intense love of drawing, as described in a letter he wrote in his later years: "The principal factor in my success has been an absolute desire to draw constantly. I never decided to be an artist. Simply, I could not stop myself from drawing. I drew for my own pleasure. I never wanted to know whether or not someone liked my drawings. I drew on walls, the school blackboard, old bits of paper, the walls of barns." In the 1880s and 1890s, McCay found work drawing posters for circuses and carnivals. Eventually, he

Winsor McCay first showed some of his animated films in his vaudeville acts. His films proved successful and McCay gained public recognition as a great animator.

landed a job as an illustrator for newspapers such as the *Cincinnati Enquirer* and the *New York Herald*. McCay's newspaper work led him to success as a cartoonist, and in 1905, he created the popular comic strip "Dreams of a Rarebit Fiend." He followed this with the even more popular "Little Nemo in Slumberland," the story of a little boy who dreams of adventures in magic lands. This later served as the basis for his first animated cartoon. Thanks to the success of "Little Nemo," McCay began touring in vaudeville theaters in 1906. As Blackton had done, he stood on stage and drew quick sketches of audience members.

Far Ahead of His Time

McCay's initial interest in animating his own cartoons came in 1909. He noticed his son playing with flip books that, at the time, appeared in some newspapers as advertisements for movies. McCay decided that a short animated film of his comic strip characters would be a novel addition to his already successful vaudeville act. At the urging of a friend, he chose Little Nemo as the subject of the film.

McCay did more than four thousand drawings for the film *Little Nemo*. Projected at sixteen frames per second, this was enough for a finished product that would be more than four minutes long. To achieve the highest quality possible, McCay invented new techniques for drawing his figures and for creating motions that were fluid and realistic. First, he used india ink, which was darker, sharper-looking, and more durable than the pencils and chalks Blackton and other animators used. Second, McCay timed the movements of his

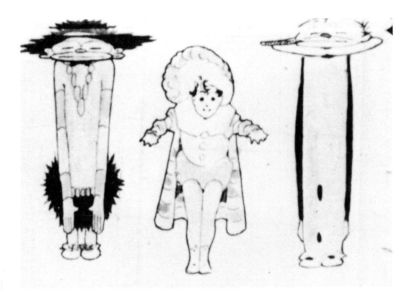

McCay's film Little Nemo *seemed so realistic to viewers at the time that some could not believe the film used animation rather than photography.*

characters in advance. He did this by acting out the movements himself and timing them with a stopwatch. If it took him two seconds to stand up, he knew that thirty-two separate drawings would be needed to reproduce the same action in the film. To further ensure the smoothness of the animation, McCay built his own mutoscope and flipped sample batches of his drawings. If a movement was too quick and jerky, he added the appropriate number of drawings to make it look natural.

After McCay completed the drawings for *Little Nemo*, he took them to Blackton's Vitagraph studio in Brooklyn, New York. There, Blackton helped McCay photograph the drawings. As he had planned, McCay showed the film in his vaudeville act in 1911. In the film, the characters—Flip, Impy, Nemo, and a dragon named Bosco—walk, run, and do various acrobatics. There are no backgrounds, but distance is shown by the characters getting larger or smaller. The movements of the figures were so realistic that audiences did not believe the film was animated. Most people who

viewed *Little Nemo* thought it had been made by somehow drawing over photographed images of real people. Audiences reacted the same way to McCay's second film—*The Story of a Mosquito* (1912). Many people claimed that he had suspended a three-dimensional replica of a mosquito from invisible wires. In one sense, McCay was flattered by these reactions to his work. The fact that people thought his animation looked completely natural was a compliment. But he also wanted public recognition as an animator.

The Lovable Dinosaur

McCay managed to gain the recognition he desired in his 1914 film *Gertie the Dinosaur*. He wisely chose an extinct creature as the main character to make certain that no one could claim he had played tricks with photographic images of a real person or animal. This strategy worked. Audiences finally realized they were not viewing a series of tricks or retouched photographs. Instead, they

McCay chose an extinct animal in Gertie the Dinosaur *to prove that he had not used photography in the film. This film helped McCay earn the reputation as the founder of the American animated film.*

were watching a film made up completely of drawings. Public understanding of this basic principle of film animation was one of the factors that made *Gertie* a major turning point in the history of this art form.

Gertie was also the first film to utilize "character animation." This is the technique of showing an animated character's personality by making him, her, or it move and react in specific ways. McCay shaped Gertie's personality by giving her emotions and showing how she reacted to the things around her. For instance, her expressions and body movements made her appear shy and lovable at times. She also displayed curiosity when a sea serpent swam by and later showed anger when a woolly mammoth crossed her path.

Another innovation in this film was its elaborate background, a prehistoric landscape through which the dinosaur moved. McCay drew the background and then hired an assistant to retrace it for each of the film's more than five thousand drawings. Meanwhile, McCay himself sketched in the individual drawings of the dinosaur. He strove to create realistic movement. He even made Gertie breathe. He first timed his own breathing with a stopwatch to calculate the number of frames needed to reproduce realistic motions of inhaling and exhaling. He then made sure that each sequential drawing included the appropriate change in the appearance of the dinosaur's abdomen.

The way that McCay first exhibited *Gertie* was also unique and innovative. Instead of showing the film in theaters, McCay made it a part of his vaudeville act. He stood beside a large screen, on which an assistant projected the film. At first, the audience saw only the prehistoric background, including Gertie's cave. Then, McCay called to Gertie and she emerged from the cave and walked toward him. The amazed audience members watched as McCay asked the dinosaur to raise her front leg, which she happily did. He also threw her a cardboard apple. An animated apple appeared on the screen immediately after McCay tossed the cardboard one. The action was synchronized so well that it appeared as though Gertie had actually caught and eaten the apple McCay had thrown.

Gertie was immensely popular, and McCay played to packed houses every night. A few of the young men who saw the show were so excited by it that they later became animators themselves. Among them were Walter Lantz, who later created Woody Woodpecker, and Dave Fleischer, an eventual coproducer of the Popeye cartoons. McCay's work inspired a new generation of young artists who set out to match his ingenuity and skill.

The Invention of the Animation Cel

McCay began his next major animation project in 1915. On May 7 of that year, a German submarine torpedoed and sank the luxury liner *Lusitania* in the Atlantic Ocean. Nearly 1,200 people died, including 124 Americans. Widespread outrage over the attack prompted McCay to create a long, realistic, and dramatic animated film of the sinking. Working with two assistants, he labored for almost two years and produced more than twenty-five thousand drawings. Released in 1918, *The Sinking of the Lusitania* was by far the longest and most realistic animated film made up to that time. The twenty-five-minute film attracted large audiences to the theaters and received glowing praise from film goers and critics alike. Many said the artwork was so realistic that it sometimes looked like live photography.

The film was important because of the new animation techniques McCay had invented while making it. To save time in sketching the huge number of drawings involved, he decided to do the drawings on clear sheets of celluloid. He called them "cels" for short. Now, it was no longer necessary to retrace the background for each separate drawing. McCay painted the background once on paper and then placed the blank pieces

When German torpedoes sank the luxury liner Lusitania *in 1915, McCay created a dramatic animated film,* The Sinking of the Lusitania. *It was the longest and most realistic animated film up to that time.*

CELS AND ANIMATION BOARD

CELS

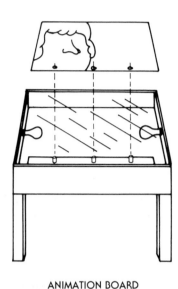

ANIMATION BOARD

Animator Winsor McCay saved a great amount of time and effort drawing and painting his animation frames by using cels. Instead of drawing a scene over and over for each frame, he drew the background scene only once, then drew the moving characters on separate sheets of clear celluloid, or cels. He then placed each cel over the background scene and photographed it. If each cel was not aligned against the background scene in exactly the same way as all the others, however, the action would appear jerky and wobbly in the final film. To make sure each succeeding cel was in the same position as the one before, McCay designed an animation board with vertical pegs. He then punched holes in the cels so each cel would fit over the pegs in the board. This insured that each cel was always correctly aligned with the others.

of celluloid over it one at a time. On these cels, he painted the individual movements of his ships and people. When McCay photographed the artwork, each cel blended with the background and became an individual frame of film.

McCay found, however, that he had to overcome a major problem with the cels in order to produce steady, smooth animation. He had to find a way to keep all the cels lined up exactly the same way with the background. If some cels were incorrectly aligned, or "out of register," the ships and other images appeared to shake or jump when projected on a screen. McCay and one of his assistants eliminated this problem by designing a special animation board with vertical wooden pegs. They punched holes in identical spots on all the cels and fit the cel holes over the pegs. This ensured that each new cel would be in register with the background as well as with the cels that preceded it.

A New Generation of Animators

In the following three years, McCay produced several short animated films, including *Flip's Circus*, *Gertie on Tour*, and *Dreams of the Rarebit Fiend*, which he based on his first successful newspaper comic strip. Then, in the early 1920s, McCay suddenly stopped doing animation and went back to newspaper illustration. Although his reason for the switch is not known, film historians believe McCay had become disgusted with the low quality of animation turned out by his competitors at the various film studios.

In 1918, more than a dozen studios were producing animated films in New York City, then the center of the film industry. Among these were the Barre Studio, the Bray Studio, and the International Film Service. A large market for short, funny cartoons had developed. Theaters regularly showed one and sometimes two or three of these "shorts" before the regular live-action movie. The public expected and demanded a constant stream of new cartoon shorts. To meet this demand, the studios each tried to turn out a cartoon per week, which required their illustrators to draw quickly with little regard for quality. In a public speech in 1927, McCay made some bitter remarks about how the studio animators had ruined the art of animation. He accused them of turning the medium into a lowly trade designed only to make a quick profit. McCay remained a newspaper illustrator until his death in 1934.

McCay's attack on other animators was perhaps overly harsh but not entirely incorrect. There is no doubt that his work was superior to anything else being done at the time.

But more important than McCay's films was the legacy he left future animators. He invented and perfected many basic and workable techniques that all animators eventually adopted. These included the use of india inks, clear cels, and pegs to hold the cels. Most important of all was McCay's introduction of character animation, which paved the way for all the lovable, silly, scary, and funny animated characters to come. For these contributions, Winsor McCay eventually came to be known as the founder of the American animated film.

Of all the animators and film producers who benefited from McCay's contributions, only a handful was able to match his ingenuity and standards of artistic quality. One of these, a young man born in Chicago and raised on a farm in Missouri, emerged from the silent-film era to dominate the field of animation. His name became synonymous with the film cartoon. He was Walt Disney.

The Early Disney Years

Walt Disney entered the field of animation in the early 1920s, at about the time that Winsor McCay stopped making cartoons. Eventually, Disney would completely transform the animation industry and become one of the most famous and important film producers in the world. But this did not happen overnight. Disney struggled for many years to learn and perfect his craft and compete with other animators. During

Walt Disney was an artistic innovator whose work transformed the animation industry.

his early years as a film animator, he developed the three qualities that became the trademarks of his films—innovation, good storytelling, and the use of realistic, detailed drawings. Essentially, Disney made a strong effort to produce better animation than his contemporaries. As a result, he quickly surpassed them. Considering the state of film animation at the time Disney began working, it is not surprising that a person of his talent and vision transformed the industry.

A Lack of Planning and Organization

As Winsor McCay had complained, most of the studios making the still-silent animated cartoon shorts in the 1920s were motivated mainly by profit. In order to turn out cartoons quickly, animators had to work fast. Supplies were scarce and pay was low. In the early 1920s, the average budget for a cartoon short was only about twelve hundred dollars. In addition to these drawbacks, most animators did not know how to plan an interesting story with a beginning, middle, and end. Most shorts consisted of a general idea, such as "character shipwrecked on island," "character accidentally wrecks friend's house," or "character chased by barnyard animals." The plot was usually nothing more than a series of visual gags. Often what animators considered

Disney was inspired by Max and Dave Fleischer's imaginative Out of the Inkwell *films.*

funny, audiences did not. Most studio animation was not only poorly planned but also executed in a disorganized manner. Each animator worked on a single section of a short, unaware of what his colleagues were doing.

Despite the general lack of planning and organization, a few of the post-McCay animated shorts of the 1920s were imaginative and well executed. Among these were the *Out of the Inkwell* cartoons made by two brothers of Austrian descent, Max and Dave Fleischer. To make these and other films, the Fleischers invented the "rotoscope," one of the few important early film animation devices not originated by McCay or Disney. The rotoscope created an animated film with motions exactly matching those of the figures in the live-action film.

The two brothers later took the idea a step further for the *Inkwell* films. They projected a live-action background, such as their own office, onto the rear of a glass screen. They then laid animation cels, one at a time, over the background. After drawing a character in a certain pose on a cel, they photographed the image and then moved on to the next cel. This process produced an effective combination of live photography and animated characters. The animated characters appeared to move around in the real office.

The Early Disney Films

The Fleischers' films inspired some of Disney's early work, although his interest in drawing dated from childhood. At the age of fifteen, Disney attended the Chicago Institute of Art. Later, in 1920, he landed a job making crude one-minute animated commercials for a company in Kansas City, Missouri. These ads were shown in theaters, just as commercials are shown on television today. Eventually, Disney tired of animating commercials. He quit his job and began making his own animated films. He convinced some local investors to lend him fifteen thousand dollars to start his own company. He hired three artists. One of them was his friend Ub Iwerks, a cartoonist of extraordinary talent. The company, called Laugh-O-Grams, produced six cartoon shorts based on fairy tales, but they failed to sell the cartoons to any major film distributors.

In 1923, Walt Disney moved from Kansas City to Los Angeles, which had

ROTOSCOPE

FILM

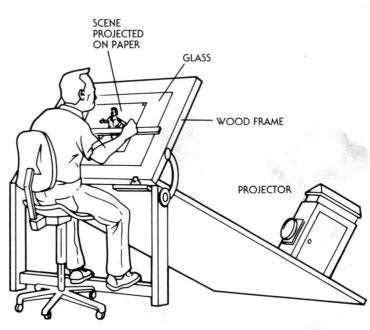

SCENE PROJECTED ON PAPER

GLASS

WOOD FRAME

PROJECTOR

The first rotoscope consisted of a wooden frame with a piece of glass in the middle. The animator sat or stood in front of the frame and placed pieces of paper over the glass. Behind the frame, a projector showed a live-action film that was projected one frame at a time onto the glass as if it were a screen. The animator traced over the figures and objects in the photo, then advanced the projector another frame and repeated the process. The rotoscope enabled animators to reproduce realistic movements by tracing live-action footage frame-by-frame.

replaced New York as the center of the film industry. With the help of his brother Roy, a businessman, Disney raised more money and set up the Disney Brothers Studio. Still inspired by the Fleischers, he experimented with combining animation and live photography. He began producing a series of shorts inspired by Lewis Carroll's *Alice in Wonderland*. Already, Disney recognized the importance of beginning with a good story. He also displayed his creativity by reversing the Fleischers' idea. Instead of cartoon characters moving through a real background, Disney showed a real girl wandering through animated backgrounds. The *Alice* films made a profit and received good reviews from film critics.

A Happy-Go-Lucky Mouse Named Mortimer

The events that followed the success of Disney's *Alice* films illustrate his talent for planning ahead and his ability to anticipate what the public wanted to see.

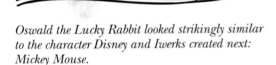

Oswald the Lucky Rabbit looked strikingly similar to the character Disney and Iwerks created next: Mickey Mouse.

In 1927, Disney and Iwerks created Oswald the Lucky Rabbit, a character both audiences and critics liked. But Disney was not happy with the low budgets that forced him to turn out films so quickly. The distributors would pay him only $2,250 per film. Like Winsor McCay, Disney was dismayed by the low quality of most animated films. As far as Disney was concerned, there was only one way to remedy the situation. "With more money and time," he later recalled, "I felt that we could make better pictures and shake ourselves out of the rut."

In 1928, Disney asked for more money per film. The distributor not only refused but also cut the price per film down to eighteen hundred dollars.

At the same time, Disney suffered another setback. Universal Studios, which bought the films, owned the rights to Oswald Rabbit. The studio took Oswald away from Disney and eventually assigned the character to animator Walter Lantz.

Disney, however, refused to be defeated. He and his brother raised more money and launched a new series of films that they hoped distributors would buy. Because he could no longer use Oswald, Disney invented a new character. He remembered a pet mouse named Mortimer that he had kept while working in Kansas City. He envisioned Mortimer Mouse as a happy-go-lucky, optimistic character who would reflect many of his own views of people and the world. Iwerks designed the character's look. By this time, Disney did very little drawing himself, having assumed the role of supervisor. Everyone liked Iwerks's mouse, but Disney's wife did not like the name Mortimer. So, Disney renamed the mouse Mickey. No one involved, including Disney, could have foreseen that this happy little mouse with the round belly, skinny legs, and big, round ears would become the most famous and beloved film character of all time.

Adding Sound to Animated Films

Disney put more time and money than usual into the first two Mickey Mouse shorts, *Plane Crazy* and *Gallopin' Gaucho*. He offered them to distributors at three thousand dollars each, but there was little interest at that price. Then, Disney had an idea that would revolutionize the animation industry. He recalled that a few months before, the Warner Brothers studio had released the first "talkie," or sound film, called *The Jazz Singer*. Audiences had reacted enthusiastically to the film. Disney became convinced that audiences would also be captivated by cartoons that talked.

Mickey Mouse would be Disney's first talking cartoon character and *Steamboat Willie,* the title of his first sound cartoon. To produce the film, Disney and his colleagues had to find ways of wedding standard animation techniques to the new technology of sound film. For one thing, because of a different projector design, sound film uses twenty-four instead of sixteen frames per second. Therefore, eight more drawings were needed for each second of film. Disney also had to match the visuals with the sound so that Mickey's foot tapping and other movements fit with the music and words. After it was recorded, the sound track was added to the film. Because every frame of film had been planned in advance to match the music, the visuals and sound matched perfectly.

Mickey Mouse whistled and performed to music on screen for the first time on November 18, 1928, at the Colony Theater in New York City. *Steamboat Willie,* only a few minutes long, was tremendously successful, attracting thousands of people who formed long lines outside the theater. Critics also raved about the film. "After seeing it," commented film historian Charles Solomon, "silent shorts must have seemed flat and passé [outdated]. When Mickey Mouse whistled 'Steamboat Bill' in the opening scene, he unwittingly sounded the death knell of the silent era of American animation."

Planning Ahead

Disney immediately showed the good business sense that would make his studio a success. After the opening of *Steamboat Willie,* film distributors from

The Jazz Singer began the era of films with sound. Disney saw the potential of sound and immediately began producing cartoons that talked.

Disney's first sound cartoon, Steamboat Willie, *ended the era of silent animated films. Disney himself provided the first voice for Mickey Mouse.*

all across the United States eagerly approached Disney with offers. They wanted to release the film worldwide, and they wanted to buy the rights to Mickey Mouse. Remembering what had happened with Oswald Rabbit, Disney wisely refused these offers. From that time on, he kept complete control of his characters and signed only the most profitable distribution deals.

Always looking toward the future, Disney began planning ahead. His goals were to experiment with new ideas and make more and better films, all of which he knew would be costly. He began by capitalizing on his already popular mouse. He added sound to his first two silent Mickey Mouse films and then produced several more. They all made huge profits. Instead of pocketing the extra money, Disney put it back into the company. He hired more animators, ex-

perimented with new techniques, and spent more time and money on each film. In 1929, he was already spending an average of $6,500 for each seven-minute short. By 1932, that cost had risen to $13,500; by 1935, to $28,000; and by 1936, to $50,000. By comparison, in 1936, most other animators were still spending less than $7,000 to make a seven-minute short.

Disney's willingness to spend more money on his cartoons and experiment with new ideas and techniques was significant not only for his own studio but also for the future of animation. In the years following the release of *Steamboat Willie,* Disney radically changed the appearance of film cartoons. His studio introduced one animation innovation after another. And Disney developed a standard of excellence that has rarely been equaled and never surpassed.

Animation's Golden Age

The era from 1928 to 1941 is generally regarded as the golden age of animation. During this time, Walt Disney and his studio artists advanced the art and science of film animation dramatically and at an amazing pace. In just twelve years, Disney progressed from short, silent, black-and-white cartoons to the film that is still viewed as an animation classic. *Fantasia*, more than two hours long, with sound and in color, won praise both inside the industry and out as a monumental work.

Disney was able to achieve this speedy and brilliant transformation of the animated film partly because he was an artistic innovator who constantly tried new ideas. But equally important were Disney's ability to hire, organize, and inspire talented artists and his wise reinvestment of profits in new equipment and materials. Instead of drawing cartoons primarily for profit, as many other animators did, Disney concentrated on quality.

The Silly Symphonies

Disney's first important experiments after bringing sound to cartoons were a series of animated shorts known as the Silly Symphonies. By allowing large budgets for these films, Disney was able to develop dozens of new devices and techniques, and he established many animation firsts. But maintaining such a high level of quality and innovation required more than money. In order to make the Symphonies and his other films a success, he needed many talented and well-trained artists. Disney hired some of the best illustrators and cartoonists in the country. They became part of Disney's remarkable pool of talent, a group of gifted artists who rapidly turned his many new ideas into reality.

One of Disney's ideas was to use animation to create a mood rather than simply to prompt laughter. Disney's initial attempt was in the very first Silly Symphony, *The Skeleton Dance*, made in 1929. It was different from most other cartoons. It had no funny characters or jokes. Instead, it depicted four skeletons rising from the grave into the moonlight, doing a dance set to eerie music, then returning to the grave. The film was a success, and Disney correctly sensed that the public wanted fresh approaches to animation.

Experimenting with Inks for Better Color

One new look Disney was intent on bringing to cartoons was color. He was not, however, the first to make an animated film in color. That distinction belonged to the Bray Studio, which produced *The Debut of Thomas Cat* in 1920. But the color process used by Bray was complicated and expensive. It did not work very well either. Colors were bland and seemed to change in hue and in-

Flowers and Trees won the first Academy Award for an animated film. Its colors were vivid and consistent in hue and intensity.

tensity during the film. So, the process was abandoned. By the early 1930s, a new color process called Technicolor was available, and Disney jumped at the chance to adapt it for his own movies. The Silly Symphony *Flowers and Trees* was already in the first stages of production when Disney decided to do it in color.

Many technical problems had to be overcome during the making of *Flowers and Trees*. A great deal of experimentation, as well as research and development of new materials, was needed. For example, when making black-and-white cartoons, black, white, and gray inks were used. For color films, Disney's technicians had to invent special colored inks that would not quickly fade under bright lights. Many of these first experimental inks did not stick to the cels, so Disney's artists relied on trial and error to find inks that would work. When Disney perfected these inks, he found that they indirectly increased the cost of animation. The black-and-white inks could be washed off the cels, which meant the cels could be reused. But the colored inks permanently stained the cels. Since they could not be reused, a complete set of new cels had to be made for each film.

Disney found that all the time and money that went into perfecting his color process paid off. *Flowers and Trees* opened in 1932 to rave reviews. The colors were vivid and consistent in hue and intensity. The public demanded more color cartoons. The film also won the first Academy Award for an animated film, just one of hundreds of awards that Disney would earn for his work. The honor and recognition of the award confirmed that he had already far outdistanced his competitors.

A Host of Innovations

All of the Silly Symphonies that followed introduced something new to animation. *Three Little Pigs* (1933) was the first animated film to be completely "storyboarded." A storyboard is a series of sketches pinned up on a large board or wall. Each sketch shows an important moment or action in the film. The use of storyboards advanced the art of animation significantly. First, they helped in the planning stages by allowing the head animator, or director, and the other artists to visualize their ideas. If an image or sequence did not seem to fit, it could be removed or replaced in this early stage. That saved the tremendous cost of animating the sequence and then having to throw it out. The director could actually edit the film in advance, deciding that a certain number of frames would be needed for each se-

Another Silly Symphony, Three Little Pigs, *used storyboards to help the animators visualize their ideas in sequence.*

Disney made The Old Mill *in 1937 with the help of a multiplane camera. The multiplane camera photographs several layers of animation cels at once, creating the illusion of depth.*

quence. In addition, each animator could periodically view the board and get a feel for how his or her own sequence related to the ones before and after it. The storyboard was such an effective tool that all other animators and even some live-action filmmakers eventually adopted the idea.

Another Silly Symphony, *The Old Mill* (1937), was the first film made with the "multiplane camera," invented by Disney technician William Garity. The device gave two-dimensional cartoons a greater feeling of depth. Normally, artists simply laid each cel over the background painting and photographed it.

In the multiplane camera, several plates of glass hold separate cels. The plates are stacked horizontally with several inches of space between each plate. The camera is positioned at the top of the stack and pointed downward through the various layers. The bottom plate holds a cel with the distant background. The next plate holds the closer background objects. Two or more other plates closer to the camera hold images of characters and other foreground elements. When photographed all at once, the different layers give an extraordinary feeling of depth. Because so many cels are needed for a single frame of film, use of the

MULTIPLANE CAMERA

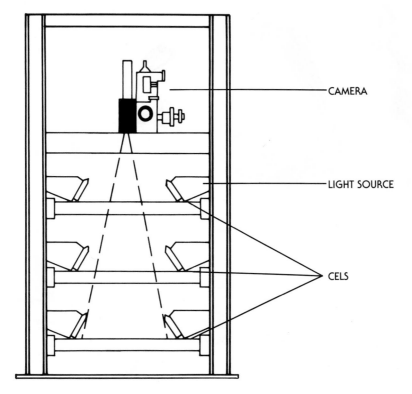

CAMERA

LIGHT SOURCE

CELS

The multiplane camera is able to photograph through a stack of cels to make animated scenes more three-dimensional. Before shooting, each part of an animated scene is drawn on a separate cel. For example, the objects in the foreground of the scene are drawn on one cel. The objects that make up the background of the scene are drawn on another cel. The characters acting in the scene are drawn on yet another cel. The cels are then stacked vertically, with several inches of space between them.

The background scene is placed farthest from the camera, the cel with the characters is placed above that, and topmost in the stack are the objects in the foreground. These objects will appear closest to the audience in the final film. The camera is able to shoot these cels all at once, without distortion. On film, the scene has more depth; the distance between background objects and foreground objects is more noticeable and much more lifelike.

multiplane camera was and still is very expensive. As a result, over the years, Disney's studio has been the only one to use the device extensively.

Disney developed many other such tools. All through the early and mid-

1930s, he and his animators introduced one technical or artistic innovation after another.

In addition to color, realistic drawings, and imaginative techniques, all of these early Disney shorts had strong sto-

Snow White was a huge box-office hit. It earned Disney an Academy Award and encouraged creation of more feature-length cartoons.

ries. Disney insisted that the story of a cartoon be as appealing to the audience as the characters or gags. He thought that an interesting and well-paced story, whether it be action-packed, heart-warming, or both, was the most important element of a cartoon. He also believed that the story should be uplifting for the audience. He wanted people to walk out of the theater feeling better than when they came in. For that reason, most of Disney's films had happy endings. Like other animators of his day, Disney did not aim his stories at children but at audiences of all ages. He appealed to the viewer's sense of wonder, to the child in every person.

Telling Longer Stories

Because he was primarily a storyteller, Disney often felt confined by having to tell his story in the short span of seven minutes or less. He wanted to experiment with longer, more elaborate stories. Also, the standard cartoon shorts of the day did not bring in very much money. Features, or full-length movies of about ninety minutes, brought in most of the revenue at theaters. Disney saw full-length movies as part of animation's future.

Disney established that future with *Snow White and the Seven Dwarfs*, a milestone in the history of motion pictures.

It was not the first cartoon feature, as is often claimed. Two silent animated features had earlier appeared in Europe, including Lotte Reninger's 1926 German film *The Adventures of Prince Achmed.* But these were black-and-white, showed little innovation, and had no real impact on the animation industry, which was centered in the United States. *Snow White,* based on a story by the Brothers Grimm, was the first sophisticated cartoon feature, the first in Technicolor, and the first to be released around the world.

A New Kind of Entertainment

Disney realized that *Snow White* could not be simply a longer version of a Silly Symphony. It had to break new ground, both artistically and technically. The characters would have to express emotions more complex and subtle than ever before. Each of the dwarfs had to have a distinct look and personality and maintain it throughout the film. Often, dozens of characters would be on-screen at one time, which required complex planning and timing. Since the film would be feature-length, it would have at least 110,000 separate frames. Because the multiplane camera would be used in many sequences, most frames would require three or more cels, each a separate drawing. In addition, the film had to have a distinctive visual style to set it apart from anything that had been done before. To capture the legendary, medieval mood of the Brothers Grimm tale, Disney chose the detailed style of old European storybooks. The artists would have to produce realistic background and character paintings of the highest possible quality.

To meet all of these formidable challenges, Disney used a staff of more than six hundred talented artists. He closely

Lotte Reninger's animated feature film The Adventures of Prince Achmed *appeared more than ten years before Disney's first animated feature, but Reninger's film was silent and black-and-white*

Disney created Pinocchio *after his success with* Snow White.

supervised every element of the production, constantly instilling in the animators a desire for excellence. *Snow White* animator Ken Anderson recalled, "He inspired me and the others with his vision of this magnificent opus [work]." All the innovations of the earlier Disney films were used and improved. If a technique did not exist, the artist experimented and invented it. If a completed scene did not look perfect, Disney discarded it and started over. As the weeks rolled by, expenses mounted. Originally, Disney thought he could make the film for $250,000. The final cost was $2 million, a staggering amount at that time.

But everyone agreed that the money was well spent. When *Snow White* opened in theaters on December 21, 1937, it was an immediate sensation. It not only re-

Mickey Mouse appeared as the Sorcerer's Apprentice in Fantasia, *one of Disney's greatest animation achievements.*

ceived rave reviews but also earned more than eight million dollars in less than a year. That made it, at the time, one of the biggest box-office successes in film history. It also earned Disney a special Oscar with the inscription:"To Walt Disney for *Snow White and the Seven Dwarfs,* recognized as a significant screen innovation which has charmed millions and pioneered a new entertainment field for the motion picture cartoon."

A Bold Departure

With the success of *Snow White,* Disney decided to produce many more feature-length cartoons. Planning began immediately for *Pinocchio* and *Bambi.* Work also began on one of Disney's greatest achievements—*Fantasia.* In 1937, Disney had started an ambitious Silly Symphony starring Mickey Mouse. *The Sorcerer's Apprentice* is the story of a magician's assistant who meddles in his master's magic with disastrous results. Instead of finding music to fit a story, Disney decided to build a story around an existing piece of music. Without the benefit of dialogue or narration, Mickey would move, as in a ballet, to the strains of the classic music of French composer Paul Dukas.

After hearing of Disney's plans for *Apprentice*, the well-known orchestra conductor Leopold Stokowski suggested that Disney expand the short into a feature. Disney liked the idea and designed six other sequences to accompany *Apprentice*. They were set to the music of some of the world's greatest composers: Bach, Tchaikovsky, Beethoven, Stravinsky, Ponchielli, and Mussorgsky. Each sequence had its own distinct style and look. And like the Mickey Mouse sequence, each was presented without dialogue or narration.

Disney spent $2,300,000 on the project and attained new levels of artistry. The subtle character expressions, daring camera angles, and dazzling colors and lighting effects in the film marked the height of animation's golden age. Charles Solomon commented, *"Fantasia* was a milestone, an animated concert that attempted to fuse music, color, sound, form, motion and illustration into a single multimedia experience—a bold departure from the stories and joke telling that animation had been used for since its conception. It contains . . . the best . . . of Disney's vision of the medium."

In just twelve years, Walt Disney had worked what many saw as a cinematic miracle. He had elevated the animated film from a series of short, silent, black-and-white gags to an art form of complex storytelling, with fully realized characters, sound, and color. His films and characters were not the only popular animation of the 1930s, however.

Disney films were not the only animation of the 1930s. Max Fleischer's Betty Boop was also popular, but Fleischer's films were not as complex as Disney's.

Disney's influence on other animators was revealed in the Popeye films.

Cartoons featuring Max Fleischer's Popeye and Betty Boop, Walter Lantz's Woody Woodpecker, and others were also popular. But none of these films were as imaginative, complex, and beautifully drawn as Disney's. And the work of these other animators revealed the influence of Disney, as the artists tried to imitate his style and keep up with his constant innovations.

Animation's golden age was primarily the result of Disney's unusual blend of imagination, boldness, and organizational skills. As animator Wolfgang Reitherman put it, "There has never been anything like the Disney studio during that era [the 1930s], and there never will be again." By the early 1940s, many animators felt that Disney had taken his highly realistic style of animated storytelling as far as it could go. There seemed to be no way to surpass the color, realism, and drama of *Fantasia*. But that did not mean that there were no new directions for animated films. Other styles, less traditional and less realistic, showed great potential. It appeared that these might provide different but equally valid ways of telling a story and entertaining people. Some talented artists boldly set out to explore these new styles.

New Directions in Animation

Walt Disney had set a standard of excellence for producing animation in a formal, realistic, and detailed drawing style. During the 1940s and 1950s, he continued to produce feature cartoons, such as *Bambi* (1942), *Cinderella* (1950), *Peter Pan* (1953), and *Sleeping Beauty* (1959), as well as many short cartoons. A thriving market for these shorts still existed. Until the late 1950s, most theaters continued to show one or two of them before the regular feature. Regardless of length, all of Disney's cartoons were of high quality, and most were financially successful.

Other studios did not have the money needed to make films as elaborate, detailed, and polished as Disney's. So they did not attempt to compete on the same level. Animator Friz Freleng of Warner Brothers later recalled, "We didn't try to do what Disney did. We didn't have the budget or that kind of talent. Walt hired major artists just to paint scenes to influence the mood. We couldn't afford to do that . . . . Walt spent more on storyboards than we did on films."

So, other animators and studios developed styles and goals in the 1940s and 1950s that were different from Disney's. Some animators tried to make their characters funnier or sillier than Disney's. Others attempted to use less formal, often abstract drawing styles to create new and different looks for animated films. Some artists sought to make their cartoons socially relevant,

Warner Brothers created a new breed of cartoons to compete with Disney. These cartoons were less detailed and realistic, but featured a slapstick style that tickled viewers.

using humor to make statements about society and its ills. All, however, had the same underlying goal—to entertain.

Striving for the Wild and Zany

During the 1930s, many animators continued to make cartoon shorts that were basically just a series of comic gags. Influenced by Disney, however, they had added sound and color, as well as better animation and story lines. These filmmakers saw that although Mickey Mouse, Donald Duck, and other Disney characters were amusing, they were not wild, zany, or hilarious. Crazy, violent, slapstick gags, like characters smashing each other with hammers or blowing each other up, were not usually part of Disney's style. By the early 1940s, some animators began to turn the slapstick style into an art form in its own right. Instead of trying to outdraw Disney, they attempted to be funnier. And they succeeded.

The best and most successful of the slapstick shorts were produced by the animation departments of the Warner Brothers and MGM studios. In the 1940s and 1950s, each made a series of cartoons that are now considered comedy classics. Warner's Looney Tunes, the title a takeoff of Disney's Silly Symphonies, were especially popular. Characters such as Bugs Bunny, Daffy Duck, Tweety and Sylvester, Porky Pig, the Road Runner, and Wile E. Coyote were always audience favorites.

The three head animators at the Warner studio—Friz Freleng, Chuck Jones, and Bob McKimson—turned out ten six-minute cartoons each year, with the help of a few assistants. They had to work with very small budgets. No money was allotted for experimentation or redoing sequences that did not work right. The gags had to work the first time. That meant precise planning of every frame of a film. Every camera shot, gag, and character movement was timed in advance according to the number of frames of animation needed.

A Matter of Timing

In fact, precise timing was at the heart of the slapstick humor of these films. Often, the difference of only a few frames, a mere fraction of a second, made the difference between audience laughter and boredom. For example, in

Warner Brothers studios created Looney Tunes in the 1940s. Among the most popular characters were Elmer Fudd, Bugs Bunny, and Daffy Duck.

Chuck Jones (left), the creator of Wile E. Coyote (above, right), found that timing was essential in animated slapstick humor.

the Road Runner cartoons, Wile E. Coyote often fell off enormous cliffs, crashing into the desert below. Part of the humor came from the incredible distance the character fell. The other part came from the audience not being able to see the actual impact, which was left to the imagination. Wile E.'s creator, Chuck Jones, learned to plan these falls perfectly in order to make them as funny as possible. He later recalled: "I found that if the coyote fell off a cliff, it would take eighteen frames for him to disappear, then fourteen frames later he would hit. It seemed to me that thirteen frames didn't work in terms of humor, and neither did fifteen frames; fourteen frames got a laugh."

Another example of comedy timing was the way the animators varied the pacing of the cartoons. The pacing of a film is the speed at which the action of the story moves. Although these films were fast-paced overall, the filmmakers learned that relentless, uninterrupted

MGM relied on slapstick violence and fast-paced action in its Tom and Jerry cartoons.

action was tiring rather than funny. It was much funnier to interrupt the action now and then with well-timed periods of calm. Film historian Charles Solomon described a scene from Friz Freleng's 1953 Tweety and Sylvester short *A Mouse Divided*:

> When Sylvester takes the baby mouse he's adopted for a walk . . . the audience sees him proudly push the carriage out the gate, around the corner and out of sight. Nothing in the frame moves for a long beat. Obviously *something* is about to happen, but what? Suddenly, the action erupts as Sylvester dashes back around the corner with a pack of scroungy alley cats hot on his heels. That moment of stillness makes the movements seem that much wilder—and funnier.

Animated Violence

The same kind of expert comedy timing was used in MGM's animated shorts. The head animators at MGM were Tex Avery, Bill Hanna, and Joe Barbera, and they also turned out a series of now-classic cartoons. They did not have a large stable of popular characters, however, like the animators at Warner Brothers did. The only MGM characters that were able to compete with those of Disney and Warner Brothers were the cat-and-mouse team of Tom and Jerry. Nevertheless, Avery and his colleagues used frantic action and slapstick violence so well that audiences laughed hysterically. The MGM shorts were very successful.

Avery recognized that violence, like other elements of animated slapstick, depends on precise timing. In his cartoon *Bad Luck Blackie*, a dog who has been bothering a kitten learns his lesson when he falls victim to a series of violent events. One by one, larger and larger objects drop out of the sky onto the dog's head. These include a flowerpot, a bathtub, an airplane, a bus, a steamroller, and an ocean liner. Avery discovered that if the audience saw the falling objects too far in advance, the gag would not be funny. So, he let the audience see a falling object for only five or six frames before it struck a character.

Avery and other animators realized that such violence is not funny in real life. Yet they saw that audiences readily accepted and laughed at violence in cartoons. People who would have been horrified to see a bathtub crush a person in real life, for example, laughed and snickered when it happened in *Bad Luck Blackie*. Avery found that the key to violent humor in cartoons was to develop gags around situations that rarely or never occur in real life. As he explained:

> We found out early that if you did something with a character . . . that couldn't possibly be rigged up in live action . . . you've got a guaranteed laugh. If a human can do it, a lot of times it isn't funny in animation. . . . But if you can take a fellow and have him get hit on the head and then he cracks up like a piece of china, then you know you've got a laugh.

Using perfectly timed pacing, sight gags or visual jokes, and violence, Avery, Chuck Jones, and the other artists at MGM and Warner Brothers created a body of animated work that has rarely been surpassed in hilarity.

New Kinds of Graphics

While the Warner and MGM animators developed slapstick humor, other animators explored new visual and drawing styles, or graphics. Disney told stories using highly realistic graphics. Other artists wanted to find a new way of telling an animated story by using different kinds of graphics. The most important and influential of these experimenters were the artists who worked at United Productions of America, or UPA. During the 1940s and 1950s, UPA brought about a revolution in animation graphics. The ideas pioneered by UPA profoundly influenced later animation, especially television animation.

Many of the artists who founded UPA originally worked for Disney. Among them were Stephen Bosustow, John Hubley, and Bill Hurtz. In 1941, they and several other animators struck out on their own and formed the First Motion Picture Unit, or FMPU. In 1945, they changed the name of the studio to UPA. These artists tried to avoid many of the traditional elements of animated films. They were tired of seeing animals as the main characters in cartoons, a staple of Disney, Warner Brothers, and others. The UPA artists preferred making human beings the main characters. For example, their most famous characters were Mr. Magoo, an old man, and Gerald McBoing-Boing, a little boy.

The UPA animators also wanted to place less emphasis on gag-oriented humor and more emphasis on social humor. There was, they believed, plenty of potential for poking fun at social institutions like the family, the workplace, and the government. By pointing out some of the absurdities that exist in these institutions, the filmmakers could entertain people and make them think at the same time. One of the best examples was *The Brotherhood of Man* (1946). The film explored a serious theme—racism. In doing so, however, its characters often found themselves in humorous situations. In this way, the filmmakers managed to both entertain and prompt thought about a serious subject.

More than anything else, the UPA artists wanted to experiment with new, modern drawing styles. They felt that animated characters and backgrounds did not have to look three-dimensional and realistic to be interesting and entertaining. The animators at UPA were heavily influenced by twentieth-century impressionist and abstract art styles. Instead of striving for realism, these styles used exaggerated or odd shapes, angles, and textures to represent people and objects. These styles had been pioneered by famous painters such as Picasso, Cezanne, and Matisse.

The UPA artists explored these modern styles, trying to give the graphics of each film or series of films a unique look. Sometimes, they emphasized light and shadow rather than color, giving a film an almost black-and-white look. Often, they drew very simple backgrounds. For example, the distant ocean waves in *Trees and Jamaica Daddy* (1958) were drawn as a single wavy line that did not move. Or they eliminated the background entirely and had the characters move on a blank screen, as in parts of *Giddyap* (1950). Another approach was to animate the characters over an abstract design, as in

A Thousand and One Arabian Nights (1959). The UPA artists frequently ignored the element of depth, which Disney had worked so hard to achieve, and portrayed people as two-dimensional line drawings.

UPA's elimination of realism also affected the way the characters moved. Since the characters did not look real, the artists did not try to make them move as real people do. Some characters walked without bending their knees. Others held a static pose for several seconds while, for example, only their arms and heads moved. The characters almost always moved back and forth, from left to right or right to left, across the frame. This kept them moving in a single plane, at the same distance from the camera, rather than moving closer or farther away. These motions required fewer changes in the drawings from one cel to the next. There were still twenty-four frames per second, each requiring a separate cel. But at times, 90 percent or more of the drawing on a cel was identical to the twenty or thirty that preceded it. One of

Tired of seeing animals as main characters in cartoons, UPA created Mr. Magoo, an old man.

UPA's Gerald McBoing-Boing *won an Oscar for best animated film in 1951. The creative film used two-dimensional graphics and simple backgrounds, proving that a film using limited animation could be successful.*

the UPA artists referred to the process as "animation with no unnecessary drawings." The style became known as "limited animation."

These stylistic changes represented a more fundamental change in thinking in the industry. UPA artists believed cartoons could never really reproduce real life and that attempts to do so only constrained the animator. Limited animation, on the other hand, allowed the artists greater freedom to emphasize and explore other aspects of their work, including humor and social commentary.

One of the best and most famous examples of UPA's limited animation and two-dimensional graphics was *Gerald McBoing-Boing* (1951), which won an Oscar for best animated film. It is about a little boy who gets into trouble because he cannot talk. All he can do is make a "boing-boing" sound. Gerald

and the other characters are simple line drawings. The few backgrounds in the film are mere suggestions of trees, benches, and houses sitting by themselves in empty space. The crayonlike colors of objects like chairs, rugs, and walls spill over the edges, as in the coloring books of preschoolers. Gerald moves in one plane, starting each scene in the same position he was in at the end of the last scene. The movement of the characters is very limited, often making them look like walking cardboard cutouts.

Both audiences and critics found *Gerald* fascinating and imaginative. Film critic Arthur Knight wrote in *Theater Arts,* "Audiences are simply bearing out the basic conviction of the UPA people, that cartoons need not be all cuteness or all violence. That cartoons can be artistic and intelligent and still be popular." Knight added that *Gerald* was com-

The limited animation style of UPA influenced Warner to use less realisitic backgrounds behind some of their characters in the 1950s.

pletely unlike anything made by Disney. There were no cute little animals or trees that looked like trees. "In this little film, all the characters are true cartoon caricatures [exaggerated versions of people], animated two-dimensional figures moving through settings that make no attempt to conceal the fact that they are drawings."

More important than its effect on audiences and critics was the impact of UPA's work on other animators. Nearly every other major producer of cartoons adopted at least some of UPA's unique visual style. For example, in the 1950s, the Warner animators began putting less realistic, sometimes two-dimensional backgrounds behind characters like Bugs Bunny and Wile E. Coyote. The Terrytoons studio, which produced Mighty Mouse, introduced the easy-to-

push-around character, John Doormat, and several other UPA-like characters. Disney himself eventually felt the UPA influence. His *Pigs Is Pigs* (1954) and *The Truth About Mother Goose* (1957) had a noticeably more two-dimensional look than the usual Disney fare.

UPA contributed more to animated films than its interesting and innovative animated creations. The studio also encouraged other animators to experiment with and develop their own new graphics. Some of these animators made the successful transition to television and brought these styles with them. Without a doubt, UPA had more influence on television animation than any other company. In turn, the small screen would dramatically change the animation industry more than anyone could have foreseen.

CHAPTER 6

Television Animation

The introduction of television in the late 1940s and early 1950s provided a completely new market for animated films. Since the days of James Blackton, these films had been shown strictly in movie theaters. Now, animation could reach directly into people's homes. But television did more than just offer another medium in which animators could display their work. TV profoundly changed the way people both made and viewed cartoons. The change was gradual for two reasons. First, only a small percentage of American homes had TVs until the early 1950s. Second, until the late 1950s, few animated films were made exclusively for the small screen. At first, almost all of the cartoons seen on TV were the shorts that had run in theaters during the 1930s and 1940s.

By 1960, however, television had become a huge entertainment industry. Nearly every home had at least one TV set, and the average family watched several hours of TV programming each day. This created a tremendous demand for new shows, including cartoons. But the made-for-TV cartoons were markedly different from the ones that had been made for theaters. For one thing, the budgets available to produce television programs of all kinds were much smaller than the budgets for theatrical films. This meant that TV animators had to find cheaper ways of making cartoons. Most of the time, the result was a cartoon that looked less realistic than the earlier cartoons. In addition, for the first time, animators began to aim their work specifically at children. This had

A family watches television at home in this 1948 photograph. Television's popularity prompted the creation of cartoons made especially for TV.

Films that were originally shown in theaters, such as Terrytoons's Heckle and Jeckle, *eventually made their way to television.*

an important effect not only on the stories used for cartoons but also on the way society viewed animated films in general.

The First TV Cartoons

The first cartoon series made specifically for television was "Crusader Rabbit," which appeared in 1949 on the NBC network. The show depicted the adventures of a small, intelligent rabbit and a large, dim-witted tiger. Together, the two characters solved mysteries and helped people.

The show's graphics were clearly influenced by UPA. The drawings were two-dimensional, and the backgrounds were extremely sparse. This was partly because the animators wanted to achieve UPA's popular modern look. But it was also because the producers had to work with very small budgets. With less time and money than their movie theater counterparts, TV animators had to find ways to cut corners and work faster. The limited animation pioneered by UPA now became even more limited.

The most obvious way to save money was by doing fewer drawings. The cartoons still had twenty-four separate cel drawings flashing by each second. But the camera often photographed the same cel several times in succession, which meant far fewer separate drawings were needed. Instead of 1,440 different cel drawings in each minute of film, there might be only 300 or even fewer separate drawings. Of course, that severely restricted the amount of movement that could be shown in the cartoon. Often, characters stood in static poses for many seconds with only an occasional jerk of an arm or head. There was very little, if any, opportunity for good character animation, which requires more continuous and subtle movement.

This use of inexpensive limited animation with simple, repetitive drawings became the standard for TV animation. The cheaper look of this animation was readily apparent and bothered many of the animators who made theatrical cartoons. Some, like UPA veteran John Hubley, refused to do work for TV. Hubley described television animation as "assembly-line stuff which can have no feeling, nor personal attention. As a filmmaker and artist, I'm not interested." Friz Freleng of Warner Brothers had similar feelings. "TV is such a monster," he said. "It swallows up all this animation so fast that nobody seems to care whether it's good or bad."

Apparently, the low quality of the animation did not bother TV audiences as much as it did movie animators. The primitive visual look and animation of the early made-for-TV cartoons did not hamper their success. The cartoons often had other qualities that pleased audiences. For instance, "Crusader Rabbit" featured pleasant, often humorous stories and dialogue, which made the show a success. It ran for two years.

Cartoon Recycling

But in TV's early years, many cartoon shows still came from the movie theaters. Although it was relatively cheap to produce TV animation, most television executives wanted to cut costs even more. So, they began buying old theatrical cartoon shorts. Most of these were in storage, having long ago run their course in the theaters. The producers of these films were thrilled to have a new market for them and sold or rented them at discount rates. For example, Terrytoons sold all of its theatrical shorts to CBS in 1955. The network repackaged these films as weekly TV se-

Mighty Mouse theatrical films were repackaged for television as "The Mighty Mouse Playhouse."

ries, such as "The Mighty Mouse Playhouse" (1955) and "The Heckle and Jeckle Show" (1956). Walter Lantz's old cartoons found new life on "The Woody Woodpecker Show" (1957).

Unfortunately, the effect of these recycled shorts on TV was different from the effect produced in theaters. Many of the aging films looked faded or had sections missing. Some had stories and themes originally made to reflect the life and values of the 1930s and 1940s. By the 1950s, these films were so outdated that many children could not understand them. Some of the older films depicted blacks, Asians, and others with ugly stereotypes. While this approach had been more or less accepted in the 1930s, it offended many people in the 1950s.

Despite their shortcomings, these former theatrical cartoons were popular on television. They were shown as part of children's shows that ran on local stations around the country. The popularity of these shows marked a radical change in the animation industry. For decades, cartoon producers and animators had made their films for mixed audiences of adults and children. Nearly

Woody Woodpecker cartoon shorts appeared in a weekly television series in 1957.

"The Gerald McBoing-Boing Show" was one of the first cartoons made especially for television. It was based on the successful theatrical short.

everyone watched and enjoyed cartoons. But these new TV formats for the old animated shorts suggested that cartoons were only for children. This change in audience targeting would become even more pronounced in the 1960s.

Television's Golden Age of Animation

An important change occurred in television animation in the late 1950s. The growing home audience now numbered in the tens of millions, and there was an increasing demand for new cartoon programming. A number of original, made-for-TV animated shows appeared. One of the best of these was "The Gerald McBoing-Boing Show," which first aired in December 1956. UPA produced the series, basing the show on its successful theatrical short. The quality of the show's animation was nearly as good as in the theatrical version, and critics praised it. But it did not attract a large TV audience and lasted less than a year.

Between 1957 and 1962, several

other new cartoon series appeared, all of which used very limited animation techniques because of their low budgets. But many of the shows were well written, with humorous and clever stories and characters. These qualities more than made up for the limited animation, and the shows and their characters became popular. This era, between 1957 and 1962, is sometimes nostalgically referred to as the golden age of television animation.

Among the most successful shows of this era were "Tom Terrific" (1957) and "Rocky and His Friends" (1959). Tom was a pint-size and entertaining superhero who could change himself into any shape. Like most other cartoon characters made for TV, Rocky, a squirrel, had a flat, two-dimensional, UPA-influenced look. That show also featured cheap, limited animation. But audiences loved the characters, especially the dumb but lovable moose, Bullwinkle, and the Russian villains Boris Badenov and Natasha. The show's humor was far more clever and sophisticated than that of most other TV cartoons. The characters often poked fun at politics, movie stars, taxes, army enlistment,

Television viewers enjoyed the simply drawn characters and sophisticated humor of "Rocky and His Friends."

and love. More than anything else, perhaps, this humor endeared them to their audiences.

In Prime Time at Last

Most television cartoons were broadcast in the morning and afternoon. This was because TV executives continued to believe that cartoons were only for children. Before 1960, no animated shows appeared during the prime-time viewing hours of 8:00 P.M. to 11:00 P.M., the time when most adults watch TV. In 1960, this situation changed. ABC introduced "The Flintstones" on Friday nights at 8:00. The adventures of a prehistoric family with an American suburban lifestyle, the show attracted a wide viewing audience. Many adults liked the light-hearted way the show spoofed everyday life and also felt it was something they and their children could watch and enjoy together.

"The Flintstones" was conceived and animated by Bill Hanna and Joe Barbera, who had produced the *Tom and*

Jerry theatrical shorts for MGM. They were the most notable of the few successful movie animators who moved to TV. When MGM closed its animation department in 1957, the two men began their TV career the same year with "The Rough and Ready Show." For this series

"The Flintstones" appeared on prime-time television in 1960. The light-hearted show appealed to all age groups.

Animators William Hanna (left) and Joseph Barbera (right) succeeded in the move from film to television. They received special Emmy awards for their outstanding contributions to television.

about a bulldog and a cat, Hanna and Barbera were forced to use the stiff limited animation style of TV. The men wanted to animate the way they had before, but there was simply not enough money. The budget for each episode of the show was twenty-seven hundred dollars, less than one-tenth the budget of one of their *Tom and Jerry* shorts.

"Rough and Ready" succeeded anyway, and Hanna and Barbera went on to make many other successful cartoons. These shows eventually moved to Saturday mornings, which became the stronghold of children's cartoons beginning in 1966.

The Saturday Morning Lineup

In that year, all three major TV networks—NBC, CBS, and ABC—began offering at least three hours of cartoon shows on Saturday mornings. Typical examples included "Mighty Heroes," "Space Ghost and Dino Boy," "Frankenstein Jr. and the Impossibles," and "Space Kidettes." Nearly all of these were action-adventure shows that featured heroic characters fighting evil villains or slimy monsters.

Television animators had always had to turn out films quickly. Now, with lit-

In 1966, television networks started airing Saturday morning children's cartoons such as the "Space Kidettes."

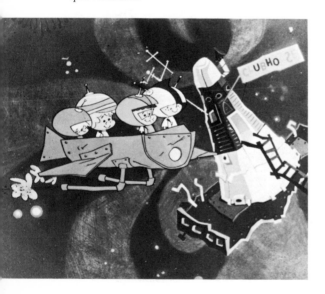

erally hundreds of half-hour episodes needed each year, they had to find an even faster way to make cartoons. Still more drawings were eliminated from the animation process as limited animation became more limited than ever. The characters now moved so infrequently and awkwardly that they were almost completely static and lifeless. Also, the graphics and stories showed little imagination. Often, the filmmakers recycled the same basic plots over and over. The quality of television animation reached a new low and did not change much in the following years.

A few of the animated shows in the 1980s and early 1990s, however, showed a noticeable improvement in quality. The animation in "The Gummi Bears" (1985), for example, was better because the show had a higher-than-average budget. This allowed the animators to take more time, draw in more detail, and make more individual changes on their cels. The result was smoother, more fluid motion and more detailed

The 1985 cartoon "The Gummi Bears" offered better-quality animation, partly because it had a higher budget than most other cartoons.

character animation. Later television animation continued to improve in this way. One example is "Garfield and Friends" (1989), whose central character is a sarcastic cat. Another is "Tiny Toons" (1990), which portrays descendants of

Warner Brothers's "Tiny Toons" stars younger relatives of famous characters such as Daffy Duck, Porky Pig, and Bugs Bunny.

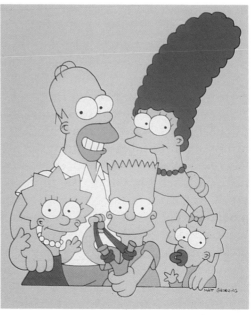

"The Simpsons" brought cartoons back into prime-time television. It features a style reminiscent of UPA.

famous Warner Brothers characters from an earlier era, such as Bugs Bunny and Daffy Duck.

The 1990s also brought animation back to prime time with "The Simpsons," a show that revolves around a mischievous, wisecracking little boy named Bart and his offbeat family. "The Simpsons" has been extremely popular with all age groups. Its combination of imaginative modern graphics, good limited animation, and sophisticated humor is reminiscent of some of the classic UPA shorts.

Those UPA shorts poked fun at society just as "Rocky and His Friends" did on TV in the 1950s and "The Simpsons," "Tiny Toons," and "Teenage Mutant Ninja Turtles" do today. Both children and adults enjoy the way characters on these shows comment on society's flaws and entertain at the same time. For example, the "Ninja Turtles" episodes often contain messages that promote personal qualities like honesty and fairness. In today's troubled world, these themes are both appealing and reassuring to many viewers.

CHAPTER 7

The Magic of Stop-Motion Animation

One of the most popular animated characters of television's golden age was Gumby. He was a little boy who went on adventures with his friendly horse Pokey and sometimes had to deal with a pair of troublemakers called the Block-heads. What made the "Gumby" show different from all other TV animation was that it was not a cartoon. None of the characters were drawn. Instead, they were three-dimensional clay figures animated one frame at a time. They moved through miniature sets of trees, houses, and rooms that were often quite realistic. On the other hand, the anima-tors made no attempt to make Gumby and the other characters look real. They were basically oblong clay shapes with sticklike arms and legs and painted-on faces. Yet they had a great deal of ap-peal, and many children loved them.

Because they worked with clay fig-ures, the makers of "Gumby" called their animation process "claymation." Although the name was new, the process was not. The art of animating three-di-mensional figures, a process called stop-motion animation, had been used since the early days of motion pictures. This was the process that James Blackton and Albert Smith claimed they used to ani-mate the toys in *The Humpty Dumpty Cir-cus* in 1905. Blackton also used stop-mo-tion techniques to make the furniture and knives move in *The Haunted Hotel*.

Over the years, animators made far fewer stop-motion films than cartoons. This was mainly because stop-motion animation is even more intricate, time-consuming, and therefore expensive than regular drawn animation. Few film-makers thought spending the extra money was worth it, so they opted for cartoons. As a result, a much smaller market developed for three-dimensional animation, and few animators learned how to do it well. In fact, until the 1980s, the field of stop-motion anima-tion was almost completely dominated by two tremendously talented men.

Gumby, a three-dimensional clay figure, was ani-mated one frame at a time using stop-motion pho-tography, or claymation.

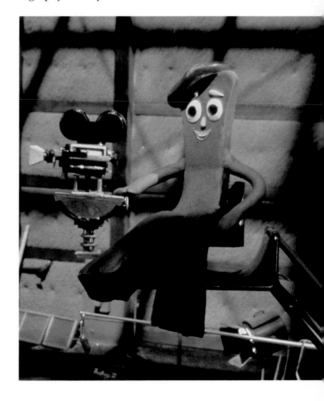

They were Willis O'Brien and Ray Harryhausen. They created some of the most ingenious, amazing, and entertaining animation in screen history.

Clay Dinosaurs

Willis O'Brien—one-time cowboy, fur trapper, jockey, boxer, stonecutter, and cartoonist—is recognized as the father of stop-motion animation. O'Brien was twenty-nine in 1915, when he had the idea to try stop-motion animation. He had never seen Blackton's films and was unaware the process already existed. One day, to pass the time, he and a friend molded some clay boxing figures. They pretended to make the figures fight by continually remolding them in different positions. Suddenly, it occurred to O'Brien that the figures could be photographed in different positions one frame at a time, as one would photograph the drawings for cartoons. The figures would then appear to move on their own.

O'Brien immediately realized that this process would enable him to animate figures of dinosaurs. He sculpted a clay dinosaur and built a miniature set made up of rocks, sand, and crude models of trees. He then asked a newsreel photographer to record his efforts on film. O'Brien placed the dinosaur in the set, and the photographer took one frame of film. The animator then moved the creature's head and tail slightly, and another frame was taken. O'Brien moved the dinosaur again, repeating the process sixteen times to produce just one second of film. He took the final eighty-second experiment to a San Francisco film producer named Herman Wobber.

Wobber was astounded by the film. The animation was far from perfect, and the model dinosaur did not look particularly real. But he immediately recognized O'Brien's genius and saw the potential for making movies with stop-motion techniques. He gave O'Brien five thousand dollars, a large sum at the time, to make a longer, more complex version of the film. The result was *The Dinosaur and the Missing Link*, a movie about Stone Age hunters who are attacked by a dinosaur.

All of the characters in the six-minute film were animated models. They were not made of clay, however, as in the earlier version. O'Brien realized that clay did not look real enough. It also softened and melted in sunlight or under hot lights. Instead, he built eight-inch metal skeletons with joints that swiveled and moved just like the joints in people and animals. He used screws to tighten the joints so that they would hold their position while he animated the models. He covered the skeletons with rubber, which he sculpted to look like muscles and skin. He also added hair and movable eyes to the models.

A Painstaking Process

In the following few years, O'Brien made several other short stop-motion films. These films caught the attention of Watterson Rothacker, founder of the Industrial Moving Picture Company. Rothacker owned the film rights to Sir Arthur Conan Doyle's 1912 book *The Lost World*, the story of a scientific expedition that discovers living dinosaurs atop a plateau in South America. The scientists capture a huge brontosaurus and transport it back to London, where it escapes. Rothacker and O'Brien agreed that stop-motion animation was the perfect process for bringing the story to life on the screen. They planned to use special effects to combine live film footage of actors in real settings with realistic, stop-motion sequences of dinosaur models.

The two men began making *The Lost World* in 1923. The budget was one million dollars, which was at least six times higher than the average feature-film budget of the time. O'Brien had to overcome enormous difficulties to make his models move as realistically as possible. He and his model builder, a sculptor named Marcel Delgado, studied the skeletons of dinosaurs at museums and did many preliminary sketches to plan the movements of the beasts. They sculpted sponge muscles under the rubber skin and added realistic skin textures. They also inserted balloonlike rubber bladders inside the models.

While animating, O'Brien inflated and deflated the bladders one frame at a time, giving the illusion later on-screen that the dinosaurs were breathing.

The animation proved to be difficult for other reasons. For example, the models sometimes had to hold position in an off-balance pose, as when two dinosaurs were fighting. When O'Brien tried to position them, they fell over before the camera could snap a frame of film. He solved this problem by drilling holes in the bottom of the miniature sets. He pushed screws through the holes and into the feet or tails of the dinosaurs to keep them steady. The screws had to be removed and reinserted for every separate frame of film.

The greatest difficulty for O'Brien was concentration. Unlike cartoon animators, who could use their last drawing as a reference for drawing the next, O'Brien had to *remember* exactly which position each head, leg, and tail was in

The Lost World *combined stop-motion sequences of dinosaur models and live film footage of actors in real settings. Although the process was painstaking, the effect was dazzling.*

The realistic animation in Willis O'Brien's 1933 film King Kong *represents some of the best work in the animation industry.*

from frame to frame. There were more than fifty dinosaur models in the film, and sometimes two or more were on-screen at the same time. Each required several individual movements between frames. The whole process often took hours at a time. O'Brien's animation was a slow, painstaking process. In a ten-hour day, he could complete only about 480 frames, or thirty seconds of film.

Giant Apes

Despite the difficulties, *The Lost World* opened in theaters in 1925, earning rave reviews and a great deal of money. Audiences were amazed by how real the dinosaurs looked. Some people were unaware they were seeing special effects and wondered where the filmmakers had managed to find real dinosaurs. An enthusiastic review in the *New York Times* reported, "Some of the scenes are as awesome as anything that has ever been shown." The film established O'Brien as a leading film animator of the day.

But O'Brien's greatest creation was yet to come. In 1931, Merian C. Cooper, a producer at the RKO studio, approached O'Brien about doing a film about a giant ape. Cooper envisioned the ape fighting huge dinosaurs on a remote island. He also imagined the ape being brought to civilization and eventually climbing to the top of the recently built Empire State Building. Cooper tried several titles for the project, including *The Beast* and *The Eighth Wonder*, before settling on *King Kong*.

O'Brien's animation for *King Kong* still ranks as some of the best ever achieved. He and Delgado built a magnificent model ape. It was so intricately constructed that even the fingers moved realistically. The jaws, eyes, lips, and muscles of the face could be manipu-lated to produce snarls and a wide range of expressions. The model dinosaurs were equally well made. Because the film had sound, O'Brien had to supply twenty-four instead of sixteen frames per second for the animation. He practiced diligently until the movements of the models looked perfect.

King Kong was a phenomenal success when it reached theaters in 1933. Another important success for O'Brien was *Mighty Joe Young* (1949), for which O'Brien won an Oscar for special effects. Like *King Kong*, it was about a huge ape brought to civilization from the remote jungle. *Mighty Joe Young* was important because it was the only film on which the two greatest stop-motion artists worked together. O'Brien's young assistant on the film was Ray Harryhausen.

A Young Man's Dream

Harryhausen, born in 1920, was thirteen when he first saw *King Kong*. He later recalled that his aunt "kindly in-

O'Brien's work influenced Ray Harryhausen. Pictured here, Harryhausen holds the head of Medusa, a character from Greek mythology, who appeared in Harryhausen's film Clash of the Titans. *Harryhausen's work established him as the world's leading stop-motion animator.*

vited my mother and myself to see this film. . . . I haven't been the same since." Harryhausen immediately decided to devote his life to making animated films, and O'Brien became his hero.

After reading about how the animation had been done, the young Harryhausen began experimenting with his own stop-motion animation. In 1938, he borrowed a home movie camera from a friend and animated a cave bear chasing a human figure across a miniature set. He also made films with dinosaur models and animated a model he called his "creature from Jupiter."

In 1939, Harryhausen got up his nerve and phoned his hero, Willis O'Brien. After he told O'Brien how *King Kong* had changed his life, the older man invited Harryhausen to the MGM studio where he was working on a film.

The awestruck Harryhausen showed O'Brien his cave bear, dinosaurs, and other models. O'Brien made some friendly suggestions for improving the models, and their long friendship began. Over the next few years, whenever Harryhausen made an experimental film, he took it to O'Brien for criticism and suggestions.

Roping a Gorilla

In 1946, O'Brien asked if Harryhausen would like to be his assistant on the forthcoming *Mighty Joe Young*. Harryhausen excitedly took the job. The film contained so many animated special effects sequences that O'Brien had to spend most of his time supervising their design and preparation. To his surprise

Mighty Joe Young, a film about a huge ape removed from the jungle, earned O'Brien an Oscar in 1949 for its realistic special effects.

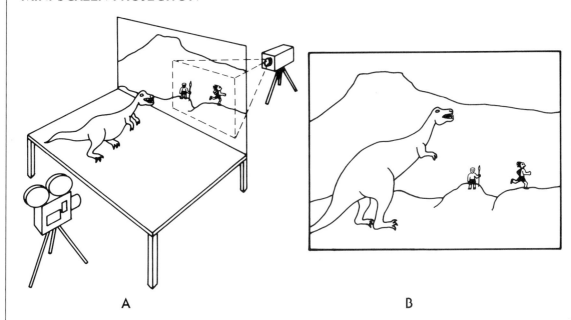

MINI-SCREEN PROJECTION

A

B

Willis O'Brien invented the technique of miniature-screen projection to turn miniature models into gigantic monsters that attacked and threatened human actors. To create this illusion, the actors are filmed first. This film is then projected onto the rear of a small, two-way screen. This screen is used as part of a miniature set that includes models of the movie's monsters. The whole scene is then filmed from the front one frame at a time (A). Between frames the models' positions are changed so that they appear to move and to interact with the human actors. This technique allows the dinosaur to tower over the humans he encounters, when it is really only eighteen inches high (B).

and delight, Harryhausen ended up doing more than 70 percent of the film's animation.

Harryhausen and O'Brien's animation for *Mighty Joe Young* was nearly flawless. The scene in which a group of cowboys on horses attempts to rope the huge gorilla is one of the most complex and realistic special effects animation sequences ever filmed. The animators achieved the stunning effect of having cowboys pass behind and in front of a model gorilla at the same time. To accomplish this, the animators combined complicated projected images with detailed stop-motion models of cowboys and horses. The results in the finished film were spectacular.

Menacing Creatures

Harryhausen's first film on his own was *The Beast from Twenty Thousand Fathoms* (1953). It was about a huge dinosaur on the loose in a modern city. The film was important in the history of stop-motion animation because Harryhausen de-

The 1953 film The Beast from Twenty Thousand Fathoms *introduced a technique which allowed the animated models to be filmed in front of real rather than miniature buildings.*

vised two new techniques for it. Other filmmakers immediately adopted these ideas for their own films. First, Harryhausen devised a way to project live-action images from the front, making them sharper than when projected from the rear. This allowed more flexibility in combining live actors and stop-motion models. Second, he discovered how to make his animated models move behind images of real buildings. Before this, the buildings had to be miniatures. The new technique made the finished product even more realistic.

In the following years, Harryhausen worked on a large number of fantasy and science-fiction films. His many menacing creatures thrilled audiences and established him as the world's leading stop-motion animator.

Unmatched Artistry

Harryhausen continued to turn out quality animation in the 1960s and 1970s. The most notable of these efforts was *Jason and the Argonauts* (1963), an exciting and entertaining depiction of stories from Greek mythology. Some critics and historians consider it Harryhausen's best work. The highlight of the film is the climactic sword fight between three men and seven skeletons. This one scene took 4½ months to animate. Incredibly, while animating each

Jason and the Argonauts *depicted stories from Greek mythology. Some historians consider the film Harryhausen's best.*

Harryhausen's Clash of the Titans *was the last major film to use hand-animated stop-motion sequences.*

frame of film, Harryhausen was able to remember the exact position of dozens of heads, arms, and legs in the prior frame. The spellbinding scene remains one of the greatest achievements in animation history.

Harryhausen's last major film was *Clash of the Titans* (1979), which, like *Jason*, recreated scenes from Greek mythology. This was the last large-scale movie utilizing hand-animated stop-motion sequences done by Harryhausen or anyone else. At that time, the fields of ani-

mation and special effects were changing. For years, no one had been able to match Harryhausen's skill and artistry as a stop-motion animator. There simply was no way, using standard techniques, to do any better, But in the 1980s, filmmakers began using a marvelous new tool to aid them in creating stop-motion animation. This tool allowed animators to achieve effects even more realistic than Harryhausen's. This device that helps create both stop-motion and cartoon animation is the computer.

The Computer Age of Animation

A computer is a complex electronic device that can process huge amounts of information very quickly. Since the computer revolution of the 1970s, computers have become an important part of everyday life. Large computers handle the record keeping and billing of corporations, schools, libraries, and hospitals. Computers are used in law enforcement, diagnosing disease, predicting the weather, and for thousands of other tasks. These versatile machines can also be used to produce animation.

Computer experts define computer animation as the process of creating visual movement through the use of a computer. The most familiar applications of computer animation are in the field of popular entertainment. Hundreds of artists use the visual images generated on a computer screen, called computer graphics, to make their own animated films. And animated computer graphics appear regularly in TV commercials, TV network logos, rock videos, and feature films. In addition, animators use computers to assist with and enhance the more traditional cartoon and stop-motion techniques. This is referred to as computer-assisted animation.

Making Spaceships Fly

One of the pioneers of computer-assisted animation was Industrial Light and Magic, or ILM, in San Rafael, Cali-

Producer George Lucas creates special effects in his films with the help of computer-assisted animation.

fornia. Producer George Lucas originally founded the company to devise special visual effects for his spectacular 1976 space saga, *Star Wars*. Before *Star Wars*, the best method for making spaceships appear to move through space was a form of stop-motion animation in which the camera, not the model, moved. The filmmakers mounted the camera on rollers and moved it a little at a time toward an unmoving model of a spaceship. They took one frame of film after each movement. When projected at twenty-four frames per second, it appeared that the spaceship was moving toward the camera, rather than the other way around. This was how filmmakers made the starship *Enterprise* speed toward viewers in the opening of the "Star Trek" TV show in the 1960s.

But this method had a major drawback. A model ship had to be photographed several times, and each time, the camera had to pass by it. One pass recorded the ship itself. Another pass recorded the tiny moving figures in the windows. Still another pass added the black field of space studded with stars.

Different lighting needs made it too difficult to photograph all of these elements at the same time. In addition, filmmakers could not get the camera to move exactly the same way in each pass. So, different images did not perfectly coincide. Ship edges blurred or were surrounded by colored lines. The ILM technicians solved these problems by mounting the camera on a special track.

They connected the camera controls and track to a computer. The technicians made the first pass, photographing the model. The computer "memorized" each movement of the pass and put the information into a specific computer program. Later, the technicians could replay the program, making each succeeding pass identical to the first. As a result, the different photographed elements blended perfectly and looked very real on-screen. The *Star Wars* and *Star Trek* films, *Aliens*, and *Enemy Mine* were just a few of the major films that utilized this technique.

Motion for Dragons and Rabbits

ILM developed another important use for computer-assisted animation—a way to make conventional stop-motion animation of animals and people look more

The starship Enterprise *appeared to speed toward viewers in the original "Star Trek" series. A form of stop-motion animation using moving cameras created this illusion.*

realistic. Ray Harryhausen and Willis O'Brien had created some wonderful visual illusions of movement with their animation. Yet their models never really moved. Their animation consisted of twenty-four completely still pictures flashing by each second. By contrast, in real life, moving people and animals are never still. Thus, even Harryhausen was unable to reproduce movement as perfectly fluid as that in real life.

In 1980, ILM devised a more advanced kind of stop-motion animation called computer "go-motion." This process allows the camera to photograph a moving, rather than still, model. The first film for which ILM used the process was *Dragonslayer* (1981), a live-action adventure tale produced by the Disney studio. Like Harryhausen's models, the model dragon was constructed to move in all the ways a real animal would move. First, the animators wired the model to a computer so that it would later move when the computer com-

manded. They then hand-animated the model in the standard way, frame by frame. Each time they moved the model, the computer sensed and recorded the change. Eventually, they had a computer program of an entire sequence of movements. Finally, a camera photographed the model as the computer directed it to move through the preprogrammed sequence.

Because the dragon model was photographed while it was moving, its actions were very fluid. Film critics and audiences alike agreed that the dragon, as it appeared on film, was stunningly realistic. Today, nearly all of the three-dimensional animation in major films is done with the go-motion process.

Filmmakers used go-motion in a different way for Walt Disney's *Who Framed Roger Rabbit?* (1988). This was the most complex and ambitious example of combining cartoon animation and live action so far attempted. The cartoon animation and combination of cartoons

Computer go-motion animation created amazingly realistic action in the 1981 Disney movie Dragonslayer.

Who Framed Roger Rabbit? *created a stunning combination of animation and live action with sophisticated go-motion.*

with live action were done in the standard way, using cels, rotoscopes, and other devices. But one effect could not be accomplished by regular methods. The filmmakers wanted to show cartoon characters picking up, carrying, and tossing real objects. So, they built moving mechanical arms that held and transported the objects around the set. The camera photographed the real actors interacting with these arms. The arms were invisible in the finished film. Placing cels over each frame of film, animators painted the bodies of the cartoon characters over the mechanical arms. To get the arms to move in the desired way over and over during filming, the animators wired them to a computer. The arms holding the objects then ran through preplanned sequences of go-motion.

Translating Numbers into Pictures

Because its uses are so specialized, computer-assisted animation is far less common than animation that utilizes computer graphics. Using computer graphics, animators can produce cartoonlike images that do not involve cel drawings or other standard cartoon techniques. Each scene of such an animated film requires only two drawings, which are used to guide the computer. First, by hand, the animator does an initial drawing representing the beginning of the scene. He or she also does the final drawing of the scene. The computer then completes the scene by filling in the other drawings.

This "filling in" process is highly complex. An image on a computer screen is made up of tiny points of light called pixels, each of which has a certain amount of color and brightness.

There are about four-million pixels on an average computer screen. The animator programs the two guide drawings into the computer by entering sets of numbers using the keyboard. Each number represents a specific visual element of the desired picture, such as shape, color, and brightness.

The animator enters other numbers that tell the computer how these elements should change as well as how characters should move in the scene. The computer then translates all the numbers into the desired moving visual images. As the completed scene is played on the computer screen, a camera records it.

Computer-Generated Birds and Planets

Several artists experimented with short computer-animated films in the late 1950s and early 1960s, but the results were simple and crude. One of the first effective examples of computer animation was John Whitney's *Hummingbird* (1967). It depicted a bird moving around and then breaking up into pieces. Experimentation continued, and these short films became more sophisticated. One of the most famous was Ed Emshwiller's *Sunstone* (1979), an abstract collection of moving faces and landscapes.

These animators found that computer animation usually looks different than traditional cartoon animation. Because the computer screen has so many pixels, it is possible to show more complex shading and many more details than can be drawn by hand. Computer-generated characters and objects often look more like three-dimensional puppets. Also, certain materials such as glass and metal have a shinier, more realistic look in computer animation.

ILM pioneered the first use of animated computer graphics in a feature film. In one sequence from 1982's *Star Trek II: The Wrath of Khan*, a powerful device transforms a barren moon into a lush, watery earthlike world. ILM technicians programmed a computer to

The computer-animated baby in Tin Toy *showed the promise and difficulty of using computers to create subtle expressions and fluid movement.*

Terminator 2: Judgment Day *used computer-generated images to create spectacular effects.*

generate its own images of the planet transformation. The movie camera photographed the completed sequence directly off the computer screen. The results were very successful. As film critic Thomas Smith put it, "The effect was astonishing in its realism. It did not look like a computer-generated image; it looked quite real."

One of the most effective uses of computer animation on film to date was the creation of the liquid metal character T-1000 in *Terminator 2: Judgment Day* (1991). In the film, this character melts and flows into various physical forms, including a hospital floor. The techniques used to create these stunning images were similar to those used to create the earthlike planet in *Star Trek II*. However, the computer equipment of 1991 was much more sophisticated than what was available in 1982. The scanning devices used to convert drawings and photographs into numbers the computer could understand were more sensitive and produced more detail. The computer-generated special effects in *Terminator 2* helped make it the most popular movie of the year.

Limits of Computers

Despite these effective uses of computer graphics for film animation, the process has its drawbacks. For one thing, a computer by itself cannot produce convincing character animation because it does not understand the many factors that make up a character's personality. The machine only knows what the programmer tells it in specialized number language. Translating into numbers the subtle facial expressions and body movements that define personality is beyond the abilities of much of the present technology. The computer-generated baby in the Pixar film *Tin Toy* (1988) showed the promise and difficulty of reproducing realistic human characteristics. When the baby grabbed for its toys its motions looked fairly natural. But the face wore a contorted expression and the crawling baby's diaper looked like concrete. This is slowly changing as computers become more sophisticated. However, no amount of time, money, or hardware can replace creative human input. Animator Bill Kroyer said: "A computer can create action but not acting."

Another drawback of computer animation is that it is complicated, time-consuming, and expensive. In the 1970s, many computer experts optimistically predicted that computer animation would speed up the animation process. They foresaw computer graphics eliminating the need to do thousands of individual drawings. Some experts even claimed that computer animation would swiftly replace traditional forms of animation.

But none of these things happened. And animators do not believe they will happen in the near future. Although the overall processes are different, computer and traditional animation both take about the same amount of time to produce. What consumes the most time in computer animation is programming in all the numerical information that represents the various picture elements. Detailed pictures take longer to produce than simple ones. As computer animator James Blinn explains, "The more interesting the picture, the longer it takes the computer to generate. . . . It takes between five and ten minutes to generate one frame of the films I make."

The Future of Computer Animation Technology

As technology progresses, computer animation for films will probably become faster and more sophisticated. But most animators do not believe computer animation will ever completely replace traditional forms of animation in the entertainment field. They suggest that computer animation will always have its specialized uses, such as producing the special effects in *Star Trek II* and *Termi-*

nator 2. Another special entertainment use for the process is the creation of moving graphics for arcade and home computer games. Experts predict that this field will continue to be dominated by computer animation technology. But in standard film shorts and features, they say, computer animation will mainly supplement other kinds of animation. According to film historian Charles Solomon:

> It has become increasingly obvious that computer graphics will not be the savior of the animation industry. . . . Rather, computer animation represents another tool in the filmmaker's repertory [assortment of techniques], like live action, stop-motion photography and drawn animation. Computer graphics will probably continue to develop more rapidly than other areas of animation. It remains to be seen whether the artists can develop their experiments in character animation to tell stories that showcase the unique qualities of the medium, the way the Disney artists developed drawn animation.

As artists and filmmakers continue to experiment, experts in many other fields are also utilizing the unique animated images produced by computers. Since the early 1980s, computer animation has become widespread in such areas as sports, engineering, medicine, and architecture. Computer animation helps professionals in these fields and others to visualize certain natural movements and processes that are expensive, difficult, or impossible to study using other methods. Such applications of animation show significant promise for helping to save lives and expand humanity's knowledge.

CHAPTER 9

Special Uses for Computer Animation

In addition to its applications in the entertainment field, computer animation is used in many other areas. Among these are sports, medical research, car and building design, and weather forecasting. The basic techniques for producing the animation in all of these fields are the same as for movies. The animator feeds numerical information representing desired shapes, colors, and movements into the computer. The computer then processes the information and translates it into visual images.

In these fields, however, the animators do not seek to entertain people. Instead, they attempt to study some of the physical processes of real life. By re-creating these processes on a computer screen, they can better understand how they work. Researchers can then use this information to improve athletic performance, find better ways to fight disease, or design better cars and other

products. The technicians can also use computer-generated images to "see" natural processes that are invisible not only to their eyes but also to the best available instruments. Because they simulate real objects and processes, these re-creations are called computer simulations. They are also referred to as visualizations. The *Star Trek II* sequence was a computer simulation, or visualization, of a faraway planet. Unlike film animators, computer animators in other fields try to create more down-to-earth simulations.

Improving Performance

One common use for computer simulations is to help athletes improve their performance. The way a runner strides, a tennis player swings a racket, or a skier moves across the snow can be stud-

Architects can use computer-generated images to visualize and plan building interiors.

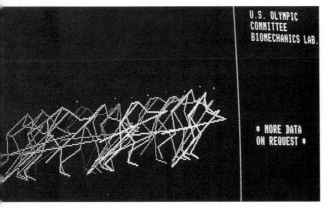

Computer animation can convert movement into images that can be studied and analyzed to improve the performance of Olympic skiers.

ied in detail using computer animation. For example, U.S. Olympic cross-country skiers sometimes study their movements in this manner. A computer converts into numbers filmed images of a skier's movements and creates an animated simulation. This is accomplished the same way that a film animator uses drawings to program a computer. The skier and coach can then study the simulation on the computer screen to find ways to improve.

This method is also used by some baseball teams and has certain advantages over the usual method, in which the coach and player repeatedly watch a film of the player swinging the bat. A film shows the swing from only one direction. Also, such swings are very fast and hard to study with the eye alone. The computer can be programmed to show a swing at any speed and from any direction. The computer can also show an ideal swing. If they choose, the player and coach can then watch both swings side by side in the same picture. In this way, the player can learn to swing the bat as effectively as possible. Players from some major league teams, as well

as many other professional athletes, use this technique to improve their game.

Animated computer simulations also help improve the performance of machines. For example, simulations are used extensively in the design of cars, airplanes, and other vehicles. Engineers use these simulations to design more powerful, more economical, and safer versions of these vehicles. An excellent example is the way in which engineers for the Toyota Corporation create computer simulations to design safer car bumpers. First, the engineers feed into a computer the information describing their proposed new bumper design. As in other computer simulations, this information is in the form of numbers. The machine displays an image of the car and simulates various real-life conditions that would affect an actual vehicle.

When the engineers want to find out how much impact pressure the car's bumpers can withstand, they run the computer through simulations of crashes. Each crash puts a bit more pressure on the bumpers than the one before it. Eventually, the simulated bumpers are crushed. To design

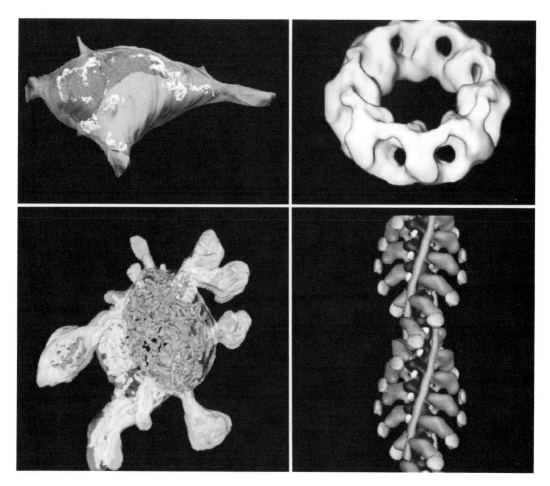

Computer-generated images of cell components allow medical researchers to study human cell structure and its relationship to disease.

stronger bumpers, the engineers order the computer to substitute a different kind of metal in the simulated bumpers and rerun the tests.

Toyota's use of these techniques is not unique. All of the world's major car and airplane manufacturers presently use computer animation in this manner. They have found that this technique saves both time and money. Before, for example, all of the bumpers and other new parts for cars had to be tested in real crashes staged by the engineers. Each of these crashes took a long time to set up, film, and analyze. And

purposely wrecking hundreds of cars each year cost a great deal of money. Although car manufacturers still use some real test crashes, most have been replaced by computer simulations that yield faster results and destroy fewer cars.

Moving Through Unlikely Spaces

Computer animation can also allow researchers to move in and through physical spaces that would normally be impossible to penetrate. With the help of computer simulations, researchers can move through microscopic realms or even through buildings that do not yet exist.

All of these unusual applications of animation are still in the experimental stages. One promising idea is being developed in the field of medicine. In 1990, Steven Young and Mark Ellisman, two doctors from the University of California, San Diego School of Medicine, began using computer simulation to study the structure of the human cell. Their goal is to find out how serious afflictions like Alzheimer's disease attack the cells. Microscopes provide a view of only one part or layer of the cell at one time. The researcher cannot see all of the cell's parts at once and in three dimensions. And he or she cannot observe through the lens what happens to the cell as it changes over the course of time. Computer animation has allowed doctors like Young and Ellisman to experiment with moving through both microscopic space and time.

The doctors began by taking microscopic photographs of brain cells from Alzheimer's patients. They converted the images into numerical information and fed it into an advanced computer. The computer processed the information and produced a three-dimensional image of a cell. The doctors then programmed the computer to make the image move. Ellisman explained, "The computer allows us to rotate and magnify a three-dimensional cell and view its components from different perspectives." An illusion is created for the person studying the simulation. It seems as though he or she has shrunk to microscopic size and is flying around and through the cell. The doctors hope

eventually to put together images of cells from all stages of the disease. They will then have a moving computer simulation that shows how the cell is destroyed over time by the illness. They and other doctors hope eventually to use the same technique to study other diseases.

Computerized Architecture

A similar technique can give an architect the illusion of strolling through a building long before it has been built. Architecture teacher and computer expert Donald P. Greenberg of Cornell University in Ithaca, New York, is a leading pioneer in this area. According to Greenberg:

> Architects can work through the entire preliminary design process. . . refining their designs and generating realistic images for analyses. . . . The [animated] images capture subtle nuances [shades] of light and shadow, and—most crucial to understanding how the finished design will work—they can be displayed in rapid sequence to give the impression of moving through a building as it will look after it has been constructed.

This technique is much more effective than the traditional one, which involves building small-scale models of proposed buildings. As Greenberg points out, "Such models are expensive and inflexible. . . . They certainly cannot give an architect or client a true sense of the perspective, colors, textures and shading that would be perceived by someone walking through the final structure." By contrast, the computer simulation allows an architect to see minute details of the building's interior and exterior. He or she can immediately spot flaws or problems in the design and quickly change them. The technique, already used in the design of Cornell's new Theory Center, undoubtedly will become an important architectural tool for the twenty-first century.

Seeing the Unseeable

Using computer animation, researchers can also see some of the invisible processes of nature. For instance, scientists are experimenting with computer visualizations to aid in studying weather phenomena. A typical example is the work being done at the National Center for Supercomputing Applications, or NCSA, at the University of Illinois in Urbana. There, computer experts like Robert Wilhelmson use computer animation to simulate severe thunderstorms. They hope to learn more about wind and rain patterns as well as how updrafts and downdrafts form. "We are

looking," says Wilhelmson, "for a kind of local rotation in which a tornado might develop." Because such phenomena are invisible to the eye, they cannot be studied effectively any other way.

In their first experiment, Wilhelmson and his colleagues used an advanced computer to simulate a two-hour thunderstorm. They based the simulation on data from an actual storm that hit Texas in 1964. First, the technician converted information about wind patterns, speeds, and rainfall into numbers. They fed this information into the computer, which created an image of the storm on a computer screen. In order to make the various elements of the storm easier to see, they programmed the computer to use different colors. For instance, they made updrafts appear as orange ribbons. Downdrafts were blue ribbons, and areas of heavy rainfall were dark gray ribbons.

The technicians watched the simulation and noted how the different rib-

Computer animation enables architects to view their finished building designs before construction actually begins.

Weather patterns can be studied and predicted with the help of computer animation.

bons moved. Wilhelmson said, "We were able to follow the air moving through the storm and then rotate the ribbons to represent how fast the air was rotating at that point. This gave us a real . . . picture of what was happening." Eventually, the researchers hope to create simulations that show the formation of tornadoes. By better understanding how these destructive storms develop, they can more accurately predict when and where such storms will strike. Weather officials will then be able to give earlier warnings and save more lives.

Another example of computer animation revealing the unseeable is in the field of physics. Scientists Horst Breuker, Hans Drevermann, and their colleagues at the Cern Labs in Geneva, Switzerland, are attempting to discover how the tiniest particles in nature move. These particles are called quarks and leptons. They are billions of times smaller than the atoms whose structures they make up. Atoms themselves are much too

small for researchers to study under microscopes. According to Breuker, computer animation allows the researchers to visualize "objects that are trillions of times smaller than the eye can see and that move millions of times faster than the eye can follow."

The researchers first smash atoms to pieces in a huge device called a particle accelerator. Sensitive electronic instruments detect the movements of the freed quarks and leptons. The instruments convert this information into numbers, which a computer uses to create visual images of the moving particles. Using this process, researchers hope eventually to unlock some of the mysteries of the basic building blocks of nature.

These and other examples of computer animation illustrate that the technique has tremendous potential. In the years to come, there is no doubt that computers will become more advanced. As they do, the programming and graphics of computer-generated animation will also improve. Researchers will find increasingly sophisticated ways to use this tool to study phenomena that would otherwise be impossible to visualize. This special kind of animation holds great promise for helping make everyday life safer and more efficient.

Inspiring Future Generations

The seemingly magical process of animation is amazingly useful and flexible. Artists, filmmakers, scientists, doctors, designers, and members of many other fields have all benefited from the process. And the possibilities for animation in the future are enormous. Modern animators believe they have only just begun to realize the possibilities of the various animation processes. As Charles Solomon puts it, "The potential of animation remains largely unexplored more than eighty years after the experiments of J. Stuart Blackton."

To explore that potential, the animators of the future will build on what is done today. Just as the Fleischers and McCay influenced Disney, and Disney influenced dozens of others, so, too, will today's innovators in many fields inspire later generations. It is impossible to predict what the animators of the twenty-first century and beyond will create. The rapid advances of Disney in the golden age and of computers in the 1980s show how much change can occur in just a few years. It is possible that the next golden age of animation will be built on new ideas and devices that people today have not yet imagined.

Glossary

■■■

animation: The process of creating the illusion of movement by photographing successive shots of drawings, models, or objects.

cel: A piece of clear celluloid on which cartoon animators draw.

celluloid: A tough, clear, plastic material used for motion-picture film.

character animation: The technique of showing an animated character's personality by making him, her, or it move and react in specific ways.

claymation: Stop-motion animation using clay models instead of drawings.

computer graphics: Pictures generated on a computer screen.

computer simulation: The re-creation on a computer screen of images, movements, and processes that occur in real life.

feature film: A full-length film, generally ninety minutes or more in length, shown in a theater.

frame: One individual picture on a strip of movie film.

go-motion: Stop-motion animation aided by a computer so that the model can move while being photographed.

graphics: Individual and visually distinct drawing styles.

kineograph (or flip book): A toy invented in the 1800s consisting of a series of drawings that, when flipped quickly, appeared to move.

Kinetoscope: A device invented by Thomas Edison that consisted of a box with a hole through which people viewed simple peep shows.

licensing: Giving or selling permission for someone to use and profit from an idea, character, or other commodity.

limited animation: A technique in which fewer changes are made in the sequential drawings for a cartoon, producing a less fluid, more stylized kind of motion.

magic lantern: An early device that used candlelight, mirrors, and paintings on glass slides to project images on walls.

miniature-screen projection: The process in which images are projected from the rear onto a tiny screen on a miniature set in order to make it appear that the images are a part of the set.

multiplane camera: A device consisting of layered levels, each holding a piece of glass on which animators place cels. When the camera photographs all the layers at once, an illusion of depth is created.

mutoscope: A more advanced version of a flip book, with a crank to flip the pages.

pacing: The speed at which the action of a story moves.

persistence of vision: The physical phenomenon in which the eye retains an image for a fraction of a second after the image itself has disappeared.

pixel: A tiny point of light on a computer screen, one of millions that make up a single picture.

praxinoscope: A nineteenth-century device that used revolving mirrors, drawings painted on celluloid, and a light source to project crude cartoon shows on a wall.

prime time: In television broadcasting, the hours from 7:00 or 8:00 to 11:00 P.M.

register: In animation, the alignment of cels and drawings in relation to the background and each other. Those that are not aligned are "out of register."

rotoscope: A device that projects images onto the rear of a two-way screen while an animator traces over the images.

short: A brief animated or live-action film, usually under fifteen minutes.

stop-motion animation: The process in which three-dimensional objects are moved one frame at a time, later simulating motion on the screen.

storyboard: A series of drawings that aid filmmakers in planning their shots and sequences in advance.

thaumatrope: A device invented in the 1800s consisting of a disk with drawings on both sides. When someone twirled the disk, the drawings appeared to merge.

For Further Reading

Joe Adamson, *Tex Avery: King of Cartoons.* New York: Popular Library, 1975.

John Canemaker, *Winsor McCay: His Life and Art.* New York: Abbeville Press, 1987.

John Culhane, *Special Effects in the Movies: How They Do It.* New York: Ballantine Books, 1981.

Ray Harryhausen, *Film Fantasy Scrapbook.* New York: Barnes, 1972.

Maurice Horn, ed., *The World Encyclopedia of Cartoons.* New York: Chelsea House, 1980.

Ollie Johnston and Frank Thomas, *Walt Disney's Bambi: The Story and the Film.* New York: Stewart, Tabori & Chang, 1990.

Diane Disney Miller, *The Story of Walt Disney.* New York: Dell Publishing, 1959.

Tom Powers, *Special Effects in the Movies.* San Diego: Lucent Books, 1989.

Works Consulted

James Agee, *Agee on Film*. New York: Grosset & Dunlap, 1969.

Tony Baer, "Getting the Picture," *Los Angeles Times*, September 16, 1991.

Horst Breuker et al., "Tracking and Imaging Elementary Particles," *Scientific American*, August 1991.

John Culhane, *Walt Disney's* Fantasia. New York: Abrams, 1983.

Jack C. Ellis, *A History of Film*. Englewood Cliffs, NJ: Prentice-Hall, 1979.

Raymond Fielding, ed., *A Technological History of Motion Pictures and Television*. Berkeley: University of California Press, 1967.

David Fox and Mitchell Waite, *Computer Animation Primer*. New York: McGraw-Hill, 1984.

Will Friedwall and Jerry Beck, *The Warner Brothers Cartoons*. Metuchen, NJ: Scarecrow Press, 1981.

Donald P. Greenberg, "Computers and Architecture," *Scientific American*, February 1991.

Jeff Lenburg, *The Great Cartoon Directors*. Jefferson, NC: McFarland, 1983.

Leonard Maltin, *The Disney Films*. New York: Popular Library, 1973.

William Melody, *Children's TV: The Economics of Exploitation*. New Haven, CT: Yale University Press, 1973.

Jeff Roven, *From the Land Beyond Beyond: The Films of Willis O'Brien and Ray Harryhausen*. New York: Berkley Windhover Books, 1977.

Thomas Smith, *Industrial Light and Magic: The Art of Special Effects*. New York: Ballantine Books, 1986.

Charles Solomon, *Enchanted Drawings: The History of Animation.* New York: Knopf, 1989.

Bob Thomas, *The Art of Animation.* New York: Golden Press, 1958.

Neal Weinstock, *Computer Animation.* Reading, MA: Addison-Wesley, 1986.

Index

About the Author

Don Nardo is an actor, film director, and composer, as well as an award-winning writer. As an actor, he has appeared in more than fifty stage productions. He has also worked before or behind the camera in twenty films. Several of his musical compositions, including a young person's version of *The War of the Worlds* and the oratorio *Richard III*, have been played by regional orchestras. Mr. Nardo's writing credits include short stories, articles, and more than thirty-five books, including *Lasers; Gravity; Voodoo; Anxiety and Phobias; The Irish Potato Famine; Exercise; Population; The Mexican-American War; Charles Darwin; and H. G. Wells.* Among his other writings are an episode of ABC's "Spencer: For Hire" and numerous screenplays. Mr. Nardo lives with his wife, Christine, on Cape Cod, Massachusetts.

Picture Credits